To the men in my life.

My grandsons,
Timothy, Ashley, Philip, Samuel, Zachary and Andrew;
My sons-in-law,
Chris, John, Rob and Mike,
and last but not least,
to David,
a wonderful husband, father and grandfather.

YESTERDAY'S CHILD

Mary Pytches

HODDER AND STOUGHTON
LONDON SYDNEY AUCKLAND TORONTO

All biblical quotations are taken from the New International Version, unless stated otherwise in the text.

British Library Cataloguing in Publication Data
Pytches, Mary
  Yesterday's child.
  1. Adults. Psychological development. Christian viewpoints
  I. Title
  261.5'15
  ISBN 0-340-52273-9

YESTERDAY'S CHILD

Also by Mary Pytches:

A HEALING FELLOWSHIP
SET MY PEOPLE FREE

CONTENTS

FOREWORD

By LEANNE PAYNE

On being called to follow Christ, Nathanael asked Jesus,
'How do you know me?' Jesus' answer was: 'I saw you while
you were still under the fig tree before Philip called you.'
Nathanael immediately responded: 'Rabbi, you are the Son
of God, you are the King of Israel.'

I have always loved the story of Nathanael's call, but for
many years wondered at the mystery within Christ's answer,
one that could allay the scepticism that was Nathanael's,
and elicit from him such a full acknowledgement of our Lord
as the true Messiah. Then, some twenty years ago, while in
the libraries of Jerusalem doing research in connection with
an archaeological dig on Tekoa, I discovered a wonderful
legend that has forever influenced the way I see this
scripture.

Tekoa is a mound about three miles south of Bethlehem
over which Bedouin Arabs now herd their camels. At least
seven civilisations lie buried there, and one of them knew
the Prophet Amos. Another is the civilisation into which
both Christ and Nathanael were born, and it knew the
dreadful slaughter of the infants as Herod attempted to slay
the Christ-child. Later ones contain the dust and evidence
of churches built over the prophet's tomb. And this brings
me to the legend, one chronicled by Christian pilgrims
visiting a church there many centuries ago.

From thence they went to Thecua [Tekoa], where the

children of the age of Christ were slain by Herod, and Nathanael, hidden by his mother under a fig-tree, escaped; and hence our Lord said to him: 'When thou wast under the fig tree, I knew thee.'

When Jesus first met Nathanael, He looked and saw the man that he had become, but He also saw and knew very deeply the child he had been. Christ saw 'yesterday's child' within Nathanael, the one perhaps still limited by the feelings of abandonment and desolation he had felt when so fearfully and suddenly separated from his mother, or the one perhaps still influenced by the terror his mother had known as she frantically hid him from the mortal danger that claimed the lives of the other baby boys in his village. It is small wonder, then, if this legend be true, that Nathanael cried out, 'Rabbi, you are the Son of God.' That is what we all do when Christ speaks to the child we once were, and allays its fears, its griefs, its sense of rejection or abandonment. This is, in fact, prefatory to the call of God on our lives, for Christ would free us from all that would hamper our ability to take up our cross and follow Him.

Within each one of us is 'yesterday's child', and blocks to our capacity to be (in the present), and to our further becoming in Christ are all too often rooted in painful hurts and rejections experienced in infancy and childhood. Mary Pytches' book, so simply and clearly written, will prove to be not only an extraordinarily useful book, but a powerful one, because she knows, first hand, that in God's Presence, 'yesterday's child' finds the divine Hand extended, the one that helps him or her to negotiate the important developmental steps that were somehow missed earlier on.

This is a book for all who would be healed, or be used in prayer for the healing of others. As a well thought out, clearly presented 'tool', it fills in what has been an unfortunate gap or void in the Christian's roster of truly orthodox books on prayer for healing. In *Yesterday's Child*,

Mary Pytches provides the basic information needed to understand the developmental steps we all must take, as well as the knowledge of how to pray for ourselves and others who suffer due to failure to negotiate one or more of these vital stages. It is a basic and therefore an important book.

INTRODUCTION

During the early period of our marriage arguments usually ended with me making the categoric statement, 'Well, that's the way I am and I can't change.' It was a depressing statement for David to hear because it locked us into a stagnant relationship.

Without change and growth a human being begins to shrivel and shrink. In fact what lay behind the statement was ignorance, firstly of the binding effects of my own history upon me and secondly of God's power to set me free from the bondage of my past. I was virtually chained into limiting behaviour patterns and seemed unable to break myself free. The years passed and I began to settle for the 'shrinkage', accepting that this was my lot! My relationships became increasingly superficial and distant; my life revolved around the family and home. Travelling and visiting were kept to a minimum. I convinced myself that I was born a loner and if relating and travelling stressed me what was the point? In any case we were all made differently.

A recent television play depicted a successful middle-aged business man accused of attempted murder. The police inspector was sure of his guilt mostly on the grounds of the man's very unhappy childhood and consequent juvenile delinquency. The inspector would not accept the man's plea of a changed character. He believed that a person only wears a mask and that underneath he remains the same. 'You carry your childhood to the grave,' he said with finality, as if that was proof of the man's guilt. On the one hand he was correct in believing a person's childhood can influence the way one thinks, feels and behaves for the rest of one's life. But he was wrong in thinking that this cannot be changed.[1]

God does not want us to be limited by our hurts and fears and has ways of breaking into the personal prisons we create for ourselves. A variety of keys opened the prison doors for me. The main ones were: looking at my own personal history and the effect it was still having upon me; receiving prayer and counselling in the safety of trusted friends; and lastly learning to live on the 'outside'. These personal experiences along with counselling and praying with many troubled people have impressed upon me the importance of our childhood.

Foundational years

The foundations for life are laid during the years from conception to adolescence. 'We know that an infant's earliest years when, unknown to him, the foundations of his personality are being laid are a critical period in his development,' says John Bowlby.[2]

The following chapters are an attempt to open up these foundational years of childhood; to look at the differing needs of the child we once were and to examine the vital role our parents played during those years.

Many people are strangers to their past history and would prefer healing and freedom without delving into the past. 'Just as we like to reach our own destination through by-passes, we also like to offer advice, counsel and treatment to others without having really known fully the wounds that need healing.' We all carry the imprint of our parents and our early life experiences within us and unless we connect with these there will be no healing. '. . . there will be no hope for the future when the past remains unconfessed, unreceived and misunderstood.'[3]

I am aware that the majority of people who read this book

will be, or already are, parents themselves and I hope the following pages may help them in their endeavours to bring up their children in the best way possible and to provide enough safety for them to grow into normal, healthy adults. It is inevitable that a book that highlights childhood problems will cause some parents to suffer feelings of remorse and guilt. For the benefit of such parents I have added an epilogue after the last chapter. It may be helpful to read through the epilogue before beginning the book and then to re-read it at the end.

I am writing on this subject not so much because of an interest in child psychology but more from my involvement in the upbringing of our four daughters and my observations now as the grandmother of their six sons. My own experience of healing and my ongoing research and prayers for answers to the many heartrending problems presenting themselves to me daily have caused me to look more closely at these developmental issues.

Though I quote extensively from such writers as John Bowlby of the Tavistock Clinic, Robin Skynner of the Institute of Family Therapy and Group Analysis and child psychiatrist, the late D.W. Winnicott, I am not committed to any one particular school of counselling or psychotherapy. As stated in *Set My People Free* I value the work of the Holy Spirit to transform people's lives, whilst at the same time I am indebted to insights gleaned from the professional world of psychotherapy.

Nearer to home I am grateful to my husband David, Jill Skinner and Dianne Harris for reading, checking and correcting the manuscript for me.

Sin and hereditary characteristics

By suggesting that our present-day problems have their roots in the past I am not ignoring our inherited characteristics and inborn tendencies. These factors often decide the way we react to our environment. This explains why the reactions of two people with similarly difficult backgrounds can be so different. One may react with apparent courage and fortitude, while another may collapse weakly under the strain.

Nor, by looking at our past history, am I excusing sin in people's lives. Many of our attitudes and behaviour patterns are ungodly and need to be repented of and changed. However, most of the people we counsel are already well aware of their sin and weep before God in their seeming helplessness to change themselves. Many of these live with temptations that they have never given in to. Two men I recently talked with have, since adolescence, been plagued with homosexual feelings and yet neither had ever indulged in a homosexual relationship. Instead they have taken seriously what Paul wrote to the Romans about men who abandon 'natural relations with women' and lust after one another. They receive in themselves the 'due penalty for their perversion' (Rom.1:27). So these men have continued to battle daily with their fantasies and their desires. I long to see such people healed and set free.

Often we struggle with ungodly behaviour and wrong attitudes, not realising that to deal with stubborn weeds they must be taken out at the roots. In some cases our present-day struggles have their roots in the past and to deal thoroughly with them we must begin to tackle them at the source.

Only the other day I prayed with a friend who had been a Christian for many years. She surprised me by saying she struggled with cynicism. She had recently found herself responding very cynically to people recounting their experiences of God. She felt guilty and repented of this attitude but despite her repentance she still found it creeping in now and again. She was correct in confessing it as sin and desiring to change her attitude, but to deal finally with it she needed to understand where it came from.

She was the product of a loving Christian home. When she was aged eleven a very zealous lodger had persuaded her to make a commitment to God by reading an evangelistic booklet with her and then persuaded her to pray 'the prayer'. When she had done this he told her parents who joyfully informed the church. The good news was announced at the Sunday meeting and a special hymn was sung. In due course my friend was presented for believer's baptism which of course seemed to the little girl to be a complete farce. She had been caught up in the religious machinery and trapped into making a confession of faith she was not yet ready to commit herself to. This was the point in her life when the seeds of cynicism were sown concerning outward confessions of religious experience. Years later she did come to a true understanding of God and a deep commitment to Him, but unknown to her the seeds of cynicism had firmly taken root by then. For my friend it would have been superficial and unhelpful to have ignored the effect and influence of her past history when dealing with her present sin.

Healing our past

However, it is not enough to understand our past. Understanding alone will not bring healing. To know and understand 'how it was for me' is only the first step. There must be a way of resolving the blockages to growth so that the journey to maturity may be continued.

I have set out some exercises to help renegotiate any developmental step we may have missed out on or coped with inadequately. These come at the end of each chapter on the stages of development. Some of these exercises can be done alone but most are best used in conjunction with a friend/counsellor. This friend or counsellor should be a trustworthy and supportive person who will listen to your story without condemning or offering good advice. However, if you have suffered severe emotional trauma as a child and struggle with difficult problems as a result it would be wise to seek an experienced counsellor to help you. At the end of the book I have included a list of some counselling centres you could approach for help.

Remember that each stage of development has taken you several years to pass through. To re-negotiate issues that belong to a particular stage will not necessarily be quick or easy. Time and patience will be needed and some of the exercises may have to be repeated and some of the issues tackled in other ways.

I suggest the use of a journal. This is firstly to help you do the written exercises, secondly to note down your thinking and feelings about the other activities and thirdly to start the practice of keeping a 'two-way' diary. Leanne Payne, author of *Crisis in Masculinity* and *The Broken Image*, was the first to encourage me to use this method of 'listening prayer' and I have found it incredibly helpful. My 'two-way' diary is a journal in which I write down my inner struggles, my beliefs, my feelings and my thoughts in the form of a prayer to God. I then wait for God to respond to what I have written. When I feel the words forming in my mind I write them down as a word from God to me about the situation which I have just described to Him. For God to speak our minds and hearts need to be saturated in His Word. Doesn't Paul say 'let the word of Christ dwell in you richly' (Col.3:16)? God uses this wealth of scripture to speak to us in a personal and informal way. I have found this to be a powerful means of healing and growth in my life.

For example here is an excerpt from my diary written while on holiday recently:

ME – 'Father, so often I don't give you a chance to speak to me. I am so busy telling you everything that I fail to give you space. This morning, Father, I have time to

listen. Please speak to me. There is beauty all around me
– in my ears (I was listening to a music tape), in my eyes
(looking at the view), in my nose (the wonderful aroma
of the sea). Outside and around me there is beauty. But
what is there on the inside? It doesn't always feel so
beautiful.'

WHAT I FELT TO BE GOD'S REPLY – 'Inside, my child, there are
imprints of ugliness. Things you have seen, heard, felt.
Open your eyes to me, consider who I am, look at what
I have made and inspired and I will imprint images of
glory on your soul. Drink of my beauty; drink of my
word; drink deeply of the love and the beauty offered to
you through others. You drink too much of the hurts and
pain and it is impressing your own hurts more deeply.
Stand apart and look more to me. The more ugliness you
see the more often you must look on my beauty.'

This was only a ten-minute exchange with God, but it gave
me some fresh insights and pointed out an area of imbalance
in my life that needed attention.

Whilst working through these chapters it must always be
remembered that God knows you intimately. He knew you
even in your mother's womb (Ps.139:13). You may have no
conscious memory of your babyhood but nevertheless the
experiences are there, recorded deep within you.
Neurosurgeon Dr Wilder Penfield discovered this with his
experiments on the human brain. By applying an electrical
probe to a certain part of the brain Dr Penfield was able
to make a person re-experience a situation or event from
the past which had been long forgotten. In doing the
exercises be conscious of the feelings and sensations as well
as the thoughts that are evoked. Allow God to bring healing
to your heart as well as renewal to your mind.

1. FAILURE IN FAMILY RELATIONSHIPS

'Parents who fail to take an active role in forming their children are handing them over to be formed by the world, the flesh, and the devil.' Ralph Martin[1]

I looked around at the family sitting in front of us and I asked myself the question, 'How are we going to explain to the children the reason for their presence in our church counselling office?' I focused on the two boys, one of fourteen and the other of six. 'Cars,' I thought to myself. 'They would understand something about cars.' Their attention was captured as I explained to them that sometimes the cars we own go wrong and have to be taken into the garage for a repair job. Sometimes only a small part of the engine is malfunctioning but it can effect its total performance. Then I went on to explain that families are rather like this and sometimes do not function very well and need some attention, which was why they were here. My explanation seemed to serve its purpose and the children slowly began to share how they saw the family and what they thought was going wrong.

Family life will never be without its difficulties and at times even a Christian family can use some assistance in resolving these problems. However the secular society in which we live puts added pressure on the Christian family. It is easy to be swept along by the tide of modern opinion. Materialism and activism can trap parents to such an extent

that financial security and pleasure are put above family life.
When this happens the children inevitably become the
innocent victims of a dysfunctional family system.

There are three main causes of dysfunction in a family:
1. A lack of communication in dealing openly and honestly
    with the basic issues of life or the unusual stresses of life.
2. A parent who is either emotionally or physically absent.
3. A significant interruption of the love process.
Let us examine these three points in more detail.

Poor communication

Time

Communication involves time. Many parents are too busy
or too preoccupied to give their children quality time. They
may offer a quick story at the end of the day but more likely
it will be a video to keep them quiet. In the rush of our
modern lives we forget that God did not give us our children
to sit them listlessly in front of a television set. Some of the
worst offenders are often Christian parents, who spend so
much time in Christian activities that they hardly see their
children. I have heard stories of clergy children who have
been driven to asking for an appointment with Mum or Dad
as both have been too busy with other people's problems
to notice the resentful glances of their own children.

Talking

Good communication is a two-way affair. The old adage
'children should be seen and not heard' may have had some
benefits in teaching self-control and humility but it caused
unnecessary frustration and anger in many children. It is
never easy to be a good listener. It is even more difficult
when the child is struggling to find the right words to

describe a petty incident regarding the little boy who sat next to her at play school. Yet many parents never make the effort and so miss the vital clues to alert them in helping their children through a difficult patch.

Other parents feel they have communicated adequately with their children after they have imparted their own thoughts and opinions about a subject or given directions on how to behave or react. Communication is about giving the other person space to share his opinions, thoughts and feelings, without interruption or condemnation, even when we don't or can't agree. Children need the same space and freedom as any adult. They need to be able to come home and tell Mummy several times how it felt to be picked on by the other children at school and to repeat it all again to Daddy when he comes in from work. This releases the tension and enables the parents and child together to evaluate the situation and decide on a suitable approach to the problem.

One morning, Timothy, our oldest grandson, spent the duration of play school standing in one spot with his hands firmly tucked under his armpits. The teacher could not get a word out of him. He wouldn't drink his milk or eat his biscuit. When his mother arrived to pick him up he went out to the car still with his hands hidden. Once in the car she asked him whatever was wrong. Timmy proceeded to pour out the sad story of his 'big mistake'. He had been doing some hand painting when another boy came up to him and told him that he had used teacher's 'special paint'. 'It will never come off,' the other boy had said, 'and teacher will be very angry with you!' Poor Tim had taken fright — hence his paralysed stance. He repeated the story to my daughter several times that afternoon. He went over it all again with his father when he came in and recounted it all once more to Jesus in his bed-time prayers. His parents feared he would not want to go to school the next day. However, the full sharing of his feelings had completely resolved the problem for him, as had the fact that the paint had washed off after all! The next morning he went off quite happily to school.

Touching

In his book *Will the Real Me Please Stand Up* John Powell points out that at times the slightest touch can say something, can convey a warmth that words cannot convey. He reminds us of the effects that the lack of physical affection has on a baby. When newborns experience no physical affection they usually get sick and may even die. Deprivation of touching can result, amongst other things, in allergies, eczema, speaking and learning problems. Obviously, touching is one of our most powerful and primary means of communication. Touch starvation or 'skin hunger' is a recognized fact of human life. 'Sometimes children ask to have their backs scratched or their feet rubbed more for the reassurance of physical contact than for alleged reasons. Adults too, often ask to have their shoulders or scalps massaged just to be reassured that someone cares. Affectionate touching offers this reassurance.'[2]

Tactile deprivation is common and tactile abuse is sadly on the increase. For many children the experience of touch has been limited to a slap or sexual abuse. No wonder a common syndrome amongst emotionally damaged individuals is the fear of touch. Babies and children need tender loving care. Love is not only an emotional essential but a biological necessity for the newborn. Without the cuddling and hugging that goes with love an infant can literally wilt and die. 'The name for this condition is marasmus, from the Greek word for "wasting away", and during the nineteenth century it killed more than half the infants born; until the early years of the twentieth century it was responsible for nearly 100 per cent of the deaths in foundling homes. Quite simply and brutally, these children died for lack of a hug.'³

Dr Fritz Talbot was once being shown around a famous children's clinic by the director, Dr Scholossmann. Catching sight of a fat old woman carrying a very measly baby around on her hip he inquired who she was. 'Oh that,' replied Scholossmann, 'is Old Anna. When we have done everything we can medically for a baby, and it is still not doing well, we turn it over to Old Anna, and she is always successful.'⁴

One of our missionary nurses from Africa was telling us about the little premature babies she works with. Until a short time ago they were kept in the warm kitchen, put in washing up bowls and placed on shelves above the stove. However, they have recently changed their policy. Now they strap the babies on their mother's chest, between her breasts. Securely tied there the baby receives mother's warmth, smells her skin and hears her heart beat. These breast-warmed babies thrive in a way that the stove-warmed infants never did. In fact, instead of putting on an average ten grams a day they are gaining forty to fifty grams daily.

Eye contact

Eye contact is another important part of communication. A child finds his basic identity from the face of his parents. Someone has said that 'a mother's eyes are the beacon light of identity'. When a baby looks into the eyes of his mother and sees joy and pleasure he identifies with that. But where he sees 'anger' or 'sadness' or any other negative emotion he will identify with that.

After touch a baby's early communication comes through the eyes. Love is passed from mother to baby through the eyes. One woman who never bonded to her mother could only remember warmth and love coming to her from her grandmother. 'Until I met my husband, she was the only person I saw who loved me, from her eyes!'⁵

Many messages can be passed through the eyes. Messages of warning, of love, of understanding. I remember when I was about eleven having to go into hospital for a minor operation. An older sister took me in and waited to take me home after it was over. The matron, however, wanted me to stay in over night and told my sister to come back for me the next day. The memory of previous experiences in an isolation hospital as a small child left me feeling almost overwhelmed with fear and I looked anxiously at my sister. She read the unspoken message in my eyes and told the matron firmly she was taking me home and would bring me back the next morning to be checked. I was so grateful to her. For several weeks afterwards I was her willing slave!

Taboo subjects

Dysfunctional families find it hard to communicate on basic issues and almost impossible on the unusual stresses of life. Death, illness, sex are never discussed openly and their secrets hang over a family like an ominous cloud, studiously avoided by everyone and causing distant or stilted communication. This can cause anxiety to build up in children resulting in poor behaviour and deteriorating school work. Children, like adults, cope better with truth than with lies, half-truths, suspicion and avoidance.

My husband's deceased sister Mary suffered from Down's syndrome. After her mother died she remained living with her elderly father, to whom she was very attached. One summer she went on a specially organised holiday for the handicapped. While she was away her father died and instead of returning to her own home Mary went to live in a home for the disabled. The family avoided telling her what had happened, thinking she would not be able to cope with the truth. After a few weeks Mary was hardly eating, became depressed and was obviously pining. Eventually a visiting family friend told her frankly that her father had died. Mary disappeared up to her room and wept for a good while. The next day she reappeared looking relieved and telling everyone that her Daddy had gone to be with Jesus. After this she quickly returned to being her bright and cheerful self.

An emotionally or physically absent parent

A further cause of dysfunction in the family is the absentee parent.

I recently heard the following comment: 'The greatest gift God gives your children is you.' Parents are God's gift to children and yet that greatest of all gifts, the ever-present, reliable parent, is fast disappearing from our modern society.

Work

Following a quick kiss father rushes out of the home at seven in the morning, arriving back twelve hours later, after baby has been put to bed. Believing she needs to augment the family income, mother leaves baby with a minder and goes back to work soon after the birth. Latch-key children have become a common phenomenon since the last war. Only last week a lady I counselled wept as she recalled her early years coming home from school to an empty house. In her memory she wandered around the house from room to room, and could recapture acutely the loneliness and sadness of that experience.

Divorce, death, illness

As the divorce rate increases one-parent families have to limp bravely along. Unavoidable death or illness can also rob children of a parent. In too many homes there is one parent struggling to be both father and mother and often sheer fatigue can cause virtual absenteeism.

Emotional absenteeism

My own father was a very introverted, quiet man, often
hidden behind a paper or dozing gently in his chair and I
never felt I knew him. I don't remember having any real
conversation with him and have come to realise that he was
a missing part of my childhood. A parent can be present
physically and yet remain emotionally absent to a child.

Depression, so common today, sometimes imprisons a
parent. Alcohol and drugs claim their victims. How many
worried children, adults before their time, are forced into
taking responsibility for parents instead of the other way
around? Too many parents have let their own past hurts
prevent them reaching out to their children in meaningful
ways.

A disruption of the love process

This is the third cause of family dysfunction. Children need
fifteen to eighteen years of reliable loving to grow into
healthy adults. Winnicott has suggested that 'only on a basis
of monotony can a mother profitably add richness.'[6] To
interrupt this wonderful monotony of loving can seriously
disrupt a child's development.

Hospitalisation

The majority of the people we pray with and counsel have
suffered a significant interruption of the love process. The
hospitalisation of a child, especially when visiting has been
minimal or even impossible, can upset the whole family.

At age three our daughter Becky spent three weeks in
hospital following peritonitis. She had been subjected to
numerous injections and blood tests, one of which had to
be taken from a vein in her neck, the nurse having been

unsuccessful from all other accessible veins. All of this was terrifying for a small child but at least we were with her continuously, saving her the added agony of separation. Children in the past were not so fortunate and on top of sickness and pain they suffered the terrors of a strange place with peculiar smells; they were surrounded by nurses in starched white uniforms and had no familiar figure to comfort them. Understandably in many cases this traumatic interruption of the love process produced painful long-term effects.

Studies on the behaviour of children who have been exposed to a stay of limited duration in a residential nursery or hospital ward show substantially similar responses. Firstly the child protests with tears or anger; gradually hope fades and the child goes into a phase of despair. These two phases alternate until eventually a change occurs and the child seems to forget the mother and when she finally arrives the child appears uninterested in her. This is the phase of detachment. On the child's return home recovery is often slow being filled with ambivalent feelings of intense clinging and violent rages. [7]

Evacuation

During the last war this left its mark on many people now in their early fifties. One lady I met had suffered severe depression for years as a result of being evacuated suddenly and without proper preparation.

Boarding school

The middle- and upper-class English custom of sending their children to boarding schools has caused many emotional traumas and severely damaged sensitive children's security. I have seen big men sobbing like babies as they have relived the experience of watching Mummy and Daddy drive away leaving them behind at school to fend for themselves. The struggle to be 'a brave little man' at five or six has been excruciating. One man told me he used to lock himself in the school lavatory and cry every day.

Missionary kids, in particular, have too often suffered from early separation from parents. Missionaries working in third-world countries have often sent their very young children thousands of miles away to school. In some cases it has been a year or more before these families have been re-united. One young man described how, as a little boy, he had fallen at his parent's feet in desperation, begging them not to leave him behind as they were about to fly back to their distant mission field.

Abuse

The home environment can also be destroyed by an abusive parent. Instead of enjoying being nurtured in an atmosphere of love the child waits anxiously for the next cruel onslaught. Both men and women have shared with me their nightmarish stories of lying in bed and praying as they heard father's footsteps that he would pass their door. They have told of the paralysing fear when the footsteps stopped and the door handle turned.

Small children are powerless to defend themselves against the all-powerful parent who seeks to meet his own selfish needs, through physical, verbal or sexual abuse.

The consequences of dysfunctional family life

Children are survivors and will adapt in order to exist in a dysfunctional home. This may cause them to repress their feelings, to change their behaviour and even to deceive themselves with lies. The unconscious aim is always to minimise the pain and provide protection against further pain.

Though these defence mechanisms may initially enable the child to cope, there comes a time when they are no longer necessary. Unfortunately by that time they have become habitual, appear normal and are therefore very hard to change. Dr Charles L. Whitfield points out that 'Children from troubled or dysfunctional families grow up not knowing what is normal, healthy or appropriate. Having no other reference point on which to test reality, they think their family and their life, with its inconsistency, its trauma and its suffering, is "the way it is".'[8]

Irrational beliefs

Susan is a single woman in her early forties. Her mother and father had a strained relationship for most of her childhood. The marriage ended in divorce when she was eleven. Not only was communication poor in the family throughout her childhood but during her adolescence, because of the divorce, she suffered an absentee parent and a severe disruption of the love process. She finally asked for help when her anxiety began to overwhelm her. She lived in fear of conflict and in dread of loss. 'I must avoid conflict at all costs' and 'I am responsible for everyone else's happiness' were two of the many irrational beliefs she held. These beliefs enabled her to avoid situations that had, in the past, caused her a good deal of pain and fear. However, the price she paid for this avoidance technique was anxiety and a list of unresolved issues with friends and family.

Overwhelming feelings

Joan suffers from a severe anxiety state. She was the daughter of an alcoholic mother for whom she took responsibility at an early age. Now, forty years on, every

time her mother rings Joan becomes agitated, feels guilty
and once again takes responsibility for her mother's
unhappiness.

Andy has struggled with homosexual feelings since his
teens. His childhood was dominated by an abusive father
and a frightened mother with whom he shared deeply. He
became his mother's 'little support,' taking the place of his
emotionally absent father. He always felt responsible for
his mother and at thirty-five still finds it hard to think of
leaving home.

Margaret has been depressed for most of her adult life.
She lives in a grey world, never feeling really happy nor
deeply unhappy. Her present circumstances are very
comfortable and would make many people envious but they
do not lift the greyness. In her childhood she lived with an
angry mother she could never please and an absentee father.
Her grey prison protects her not only from the many painful
feelings locked up within her but also from the risk of
looking forward to good things happening and then
suffering the pain of being disappointed.

Unhealthy behaviour patterns

People use behaviour to defend against pain. Betty's mother
was often unreliable and sometimes cruel. Her first and most
important attachment experience was therefore a painful
one. In her childish wisdom she decided that relating
demanded too high a price. Her consequent behaviour was
never to attach to anyone. Her lonely adult world now
consists of many acquaintances but no intimate friends.

Breaking free

Understanding one's own personal history is the first step
in helping a person to break free from its damaging effects.
'We first have to identify our losses or traumas. Then we

can begin to re-experience them, going through our grief work and completing it, rather than trying to go around it or trying to avoid it as we have been doing up until now.'[9]

Understanding may be the first step in our healing, but grieving for the lost parts of our childhood is the next important step. For this reason the exercises at the end of each chapter encourage this grief work. A person in depression is sometimes mistakenly thought to be mourning. Alice Miller suggests that 'Depression leads him close to his wounds, but only the mourning for what he has missed, missed at the crucial time, can lead to real healing.'[10] True grieving uncovers the wounds and mourns them with painful energy until healing is achieved. Depression, though close to the wounds, covers them with a grey blanket and brings no sense of release.

To help our understanding I will map out the different stages of development, looking at the challenges that face both parents and child at each stage. When a particular stage has not been negotiated adequately a person has the tendency to be 'stuck' or 'blocked' in a specific aspect of life. If, for example, the task of learning to trust is not achieved in the first year of life, mistrust will result and may become a permanent pattern of life. One stage leads on to another and each has within it features of earlier stages, 'the final stage of one sequence becoming the first of the next.'[11]

By charting a child's progress in this way we realise that every child is an individual and has his own map to follow, his own development being fluid and personal. However, generally speaking a normal child will follow the pattern outlined with the difference of a few months in either direction. Before taking this detailed look at family life I will set the scene by examining briefly the parental roles and the model for family relationships which I feel most coincide with God's purpose and plan.

Exercises

Before beginning these exercises be sure you have at least half an hour in which to do the written ones. When working with your friend or counsellor make sure you have an uninterrupted hour and don't be afraid of repeating an exercise several times.

1. Write in your diary a description of your family. Use one adjective to describe each member.
For example: My mother was loving, or my mother was depressed.

2. According to John Powell the five levels of communication are as follows:
   1. Cliche level – The weather, etc.
   2. Reporting facts – News items.
   3. Sharing opinions – Ideas and beliefs about life.
   4. Sharing feelings – I feel anxious, angry, happy, etc.
   5. Total honesty and openness.
   At which level did your family normally communicate? At which level do you comfortably communicate now?

3. Answer the following questions.
Were your father and mother there for you physically?
Were they there for you emotionally?
Were your father or your mother abusive?
Did they drink or take drugs?

4. Describe, in your diary, any known interruption of the love process.

5. Share your responses to the above questions with a friend/counsellor.

6. Together bring any unresolved issues to God. Usually a sense of loss will accompany any negative experience. Allow yourself to grieve any loss in your childhood. It may be a loss of a relationship, of fun, of being carefree, or a loss

of innocence.

When you have fully grieved the loss you will find it easier to forgive from your heart those who caused the hurt.

7. Remember the importance Jesus gave to forgiveness. If this is unclear to you spend time meditating on the Story of the Unmerciful Servant in Matt.18:21–35. Look particularly at the end of the story. 'In anger his master turned him over to the jailers to be tortured, until he should pay back all he owed. This is how my heavenly Father will treat each of you unless you forgive your brother from your heart.'

Also when Jesus taught the Lord's Prayer to his disciples he enlarged on the need to forgive. 'Forgive us our debts, as we also have forgiven our debtors . . . For if you forgive men when they sin against you, your heavenly Father will also forgive you. But if you do not forgive men their sins, your Father will not forgive your sins' (Matt.6:12,14,15).

8. Ask God to show you any irrational thinking or unhealthy behaviour patterns that may have developed as a result of your dysfunctional family background. Use your diary to confess these to God and ask Him to replace the lies with His truth and to show you the necessary changes He requires in your behaviour. Give Him time to speak to you and then write down what He says to you. 'When he, the Spirit of truth, comes, he will guide you into all truth' (Jn.16:13). 'Then you will know the truth, and the truth will set you free' (Jn.8:32).

9. 'You (God) open your hand and satisfy the desires of every living thing' (Ps.145:16).

Close your eyes and visualise your Heavenly Father with His hands stretched out towards you. He has a present in His hands for you. Draw near to Him and see what He wants to give you. Take the gift and let it be the beginning of healing in your heart.

2. A BIBLICAL PATTERN FOR THE FAMILY

'So God created man in his own image, in the image
of God he created him; male and female he created
them' (Gen.1:27).

In the prayer of Jesus, recorded for us by St John, Jesus prays
for his disciples who are not of the world though they are still
in the world. He prays not that they are taken out of the world
but that they are protected from the evil one (Jn.17).

It was an important prayer for the disciples then but the
danger is not over and we still need that protection around
us today. We are in the world but not of it. Secular values
will always confront and seek to intrude in any Christian
family. Left unguarded, the family may quickly be
penetrated by these worldly values. It is important therefore
to continually examine the protection around our family life
and seek ways of maintaining and strengthening it.

Many Christians perpetuate the dysfunctional family life
in which they have grown up. They have become Christians
but continue to be ruled by the standards, patterns and values
of the world around them. The reason for this control lies
partly in their need for healing and transformation, but is also
due to the lack of clear teaching and guidance on family life.

The family unit

When trying to give a family group a picture of how a family functions or can malfunction I have used the metaphor of a car (as I mentioned in the previous chapter). This can be helpful but in many ways falls short of an adequate description. For one thing a family is a living organism, constantly moving, changing and growing. Robin Skynner in his book *One Flesh, Separate Persons* explains the family as a system, using the general systems theory. The family is depicted as a system within the larger system of the community. Around each system is a protective boundary. This boundary is like a skin or outer edge which keeps the family intact as a separate entity within the community. It touches and may be influenced by other systems and the larger system but the boundary should prevent it being absorbed or damaged by either the community system or other family systems around it.

The need for healthy boundaries is illustrated by what is happening to the ozone layer. This layer acts as a boundary around the world, preventing destructive rays from the sun penetrating our planet. According to scientists this boundary has not been properly maintained; holes are appearing and here on earth we are beginning to suffer serious consequences in many different ways.

Boundaries are a necessary part of life. They provide protection and control. God put boundaries around His people when He gave them the ten commandments. Jude also encourages Christians to 'Stay always within the boundaries where God's love can reach and bless you' (v.21, Living Bible). The boundary around the family system provides the freedom and protection for the work of care, nurture, growth and development to occur unheeded within the family. However, someone is needed to maintain the boundary and another person to perform the work within it.

Distinct functions

Growth is a process and takes time. For it to be accomplished many stages of development have to be passed through. Within the family there is work to be done, tasks to be achieved, skills to be learned. Maintaining the boundary around the family, deciding what to permit to pass through from outside to inside and what to restrict or refuse entrance, facilitates this happening. The boundary is there to maintain a fixed structure; to prevent it disintegrating or becoming misshapen or even absorbed by other structures outside. At the same time, however, it must facilitate maximum movement and growth within the structure.

Bridges are needed as the family develops to enable members to cross backwards and forwards from inside to outside. The use of these bridges has to be controlled and carefully monitored and will change according to the health of the family, the stage of development and the tolerance of the family to outside influences. Boundary maintenance, bridge building and restricting the flow of material crossing into and out of the family are important functions. All this work has to be done or at least initiated and controlled by somebody.

When these tasks are adequately performed then the day-to-day work inside the family structure can be carried on without too much outside disturbance and distraction. Inside the system there is the daily work of nurturing and caring to be done, of teaching basic skills and the work of character formation. This requires a constant, reliable presence.

Both the task of maintaining and guarding the boundary and the task of nurture and formation are vital and necessary for the healthy development of the individual members. Neither task is subservient to, or independent of, the other and at times they are interchangeable. Despite some modern opinions it would seem that the male is naturally more able to perform one function and the female the other.

Gender differences

When God created mankind He made male and female. 'So God created man in his own image, in the image of God he created him; male and female he created them. God blessed them and said to them, "Be fruitful and increase in number" ' (Gen.1:27,28). Later God said, 'For this reason a man will leave his father and mother and will be united to his wife and they will become one flesh' (Gen.2:24).

The human family starts with a man and a woman leaving their family of origin and coming together as one flesh and out of that union children are born. Yet physically and emotionally men and women are different. Generally speaking we fall naturally into the role of male and female. The male is built to penetrate and the female to be penetrated. 'Adam (or The Man) lay with his wife Eve, and she conceived and gave birth to Cain' (Gen. 4:1). The female has a womb in which to house a baby for nine months. The male does not. After the baby is born the female produces milk, perfect in content, to feed and nurture a baby for many months. The male is not able to do this either. The woman therefore is perfectly made to perform the more nurturing and caring tasks inside the family boundary. But to give herself to this task adequately she needs a partner to take up the work of maintaining and guarding the boundary around her and the child she is nurturing. The male is ideally suited and equipped to do this — both physically and emotionally.

After twenty years of clinical experience Robin Skynner is convinced that 'the optimal pattern for family functioning is one in which the father in general accepts the ultimate responsibility and the authority which goes with this'. Though this view is widely shared amongst family therapists it is not always freely acknowledged. Skynner says that 'Some North American family therapists avoid expressing such views openly in the present climate of opinion.'[1] In other words they are afraid of reaction from the feminists.

God judged Eli the priest for failing to restrain his sons who had sinned by 'treating the Lord's offering with contempt' (1 Sam.2:17). He had been a slack father and had not maintained the boundaries around his family. For this reason God took the priesthood from Eli's family. God's desire is for the family to be protected and disciplined by a strong father figure.

Instructing Timothy in the choice of an overseer for the church, Paul says that he must be a man who can 'manage his own family well and see that his children obey him with proper respect'. A deacon likewise 'must manage his children and his household well' (1 Tim.3:4,12).

The secular society in which we live continually undermines the traditional, biblical view of family life and many Christians flounder under the pressure to conform to the standards of the world. We recently visited a vibrant and fast-growing Christian fellowship in Kansas City, USA. Their members stood out in sharp contrast to the materialistic society around them. They had adopted a simple life style, which freed the mother to be at home with the children, instead of feeling pressurised to go out to work and earn more money. They also placed a very high value on family life and I noticed especially the important role the father played in this.

When God created male and female he created two kinds of people. They were not identical but were created with differences which indicated distinct functions. The man's first instruction from God was to rule over His creation (Gen.1:26). Secondly he was told to go and produce a family (Gen.1:28). The woman's primary function, however, was to be a helper 'suitable' for the man (Gen.2:18). Later Adam obeyed God's injunction to be fruitful and multiply and he 'lay with his wife Eve, and she conceived and gave birth to Cain' (Gen.4:1).

The servant leader

For the father to perform his task adequately he must have the capacity to be aware of the individual as well as the corporate needs of the family. As a good leader he must be able to lay aside his own needs for the sake of others. Paul exhorts husbands to love their wives as 'Christ loved the church and gave himself up for her' (Eph.5:25). Jesus sacrificially laid aside his own needs, his own life for the benefit and service of his bride, the church. He thus exemplified the role of servant/leader for every husband and head of family.

God sent his own beloved son into the world as a small baby. He chose Mary to carry his son and to nurture him. He chose Joseph to protect and guard him.

At Christmas time we receive cards depicting various aspects of the Christmas story. These traditional nativity scenarios convey the concept quite naturally. On one we see Mary and Joseph arriving at Bethlehem, Mary on the donkey, heavy with child, Joseph looking for a shelter in which she can have the baby. Another shows the stable with Mary holding the babe in her arms while Joseph stands behind, guarding and protecting his little family. Or it may be a picture of the family fleeing to Egypt after Joseph has been warned about King Herod's threats to kill Jesus. Again Joseph is protecting and providing for his family as instructed by God.

The birth of Jesus is surrounded with angelic appearances and warning dreams. Only once does Mary receive a visitation and that is to foretell the birth of Jesus (Luke 1:28). Thereafter the visitations and dreams are to others and amongst them Joseph receives four important messages, each time to guide him in his job as guardian of the family. In the first dream the Lord commands him to take Mary as his wife and so ensures His son the security of a mother and a father (Matt.1:20). Secondly an angel appears to tell

Joseph to escape to Egypt (Matt.2:13) and later an angel appears to tell him it is now safe to return (Matt.2:20). Lastly another dream warns Joseph that Archelaus is reigning in Judea in place of his father Herod, so he goes to live in Galilee instead (Matt.2:22). Each time we notice that God speaks to Joseph, not Mary, placing him at the boundary of the family in the position of guardian and protector.

The importance of gender difference

Allowing for some necessary overlapping and helping out, the whole family functions best where father and mother naturally and easily adopt their distinctive roles. Individual children within the family clearly benefit where these roles are defined. 'There seems at least to be general agreement,' writes Skynner, 'that clear and unambiguous differentiation of the two gender roles within a marriage is necessary if the children are to develop without a harmful degree of confusion and conflict.'[2] Children receive their sexual identity from their parents. They have both male and female roles modelled before them. Girls will identify with mother and boys with father, where the differentiation is clearly defined.

Another benefit derived from the distinct roles is that when father takes up the position of authority and responsibility there is a clear understanding by everyone of who is in control. The children feel more secure and have greater freedom to explore within the boundary knowing there is a limit beyond which they cannot go.

In our own family, with four children very close to each other in age, authority and control were important factors for keeping a happy atmosphere. As mother my hands were full with the more nurturing job of feeding, washing, clothing and comforting. David took charge of the boundaries, defining and controlling them. He provided a secure environment for happy relating. When he was forced to be away for any length of time, I realised how difficult it was trying to fill both roles. One Sunday, after a whole weekend without David, I remember sitting on the bottom step of the stairs and sobbing with frustration and tiredness. Above me four little heads were peeping through the banisters and looking down on me with awe. They knew they had pushed me too far and probably longed as much as I did for Daddy to come home and restore law and order to a situation fast becoming uncomfortably out of control.

Confusion and conflict over the parent's sexual identity, lack of secure boundaries and too little nurturing can be the cause of many problems in childhood resulting later in ambivalent sexual identity, anxiety and insecurity. Where such ill-prepared adults marry and set up home they will often find themselves unable to provide a healthy functional family system not having themselves experienced one. History will continue to repeat itself. But the good news is that the vicious cycle can be broken. The road to healing and change, however, commences when we begin to understand our own personal history and can recognise the unfinished developmental tasks left over from our childhood.

Parental roles will continue to be a focal point in the following pages as we look more closely at the beginnings of family life.

Exercises

1. In your imagination see yourself as you were at eight years of age. Go to the sitting room in your family home.

First see your father come into the room.

How do you feel when you see him?

What does he do when he enters the room?

Now see your mother come into the room.
How do you feel when you see her?
What does she do?

2. Visualise your whole family gathered around the table for a meal.
Where is your father sitting?
Where is your mother sitting?
What are they doing?
What are they saying?
How does this make you feel?

3. These memories may have given you only good and happy feelings. In this case thank God for your family life. However, the memories may have stirred some uncomfortable, even painful feelings. If this is so, you will certainly have received a poor model of family life and of parental roles, and these will need changing. Ask the Holy Spirit to come and begin this work of transformation now.

4. In your imagination picture the stable where Jesus was born. See Mary nurturing and caring for the baby. See Joseph standing guard over the mother and child, protecting them from harm. Take in the rightness of this picture and thank God for His perfect plan for families. Spend time dwelling on this picture and letting it take root within you.

5. 'For he has rescued us from the dominion of darkness and brought us into the kingdom of the Son he loves . . .' (Col.1:13). Your family of origin may have been very dysfunctional and you have received hurts as a result. Remember you have been taken out of that darkness and been brought into a new family. You have been invited to share in the security of the loving relationship between the Father and the Son.

6. Spend some time reflecting and meditating on this relationship. See yourself sharing in it and start allowing yourself to enjoy and benefit from it.

3.   THE SECRET PLACE
(In the Womb)

'Heavenly Father, maker of all things, you enable
us to share in your work of creation. Bless this
couple in the gift and care of children, that their
home may be a place of love, security, and truth,
and their children grow up to know and love you
in your Son Jesus Christ our Lord. Amen.' (A
prayer from the Marriage Service of the Church of
England. A.S.B.)

Babies were intended to be the fruit of a dependable, loving
commitment between a man and a woman. Into such a
secure environment children can be welcomed and given the
best possible chance to develop into normal healthy adults.
However, we have to realise that conception may take place
in many different circumstances and for many different
reasons. It may take place in the context of tender self-giving
love or selfish and brutal lust. Conception may occur either
inside or outside the bonds of marriage. It may come
through careful planning or by careless accident. In whatever
way it happens an incredible miracle takes place in that
moment of time. A human life, with all its potential, is
conceived.

Between the moment of baby's conception and the
moment of realisation by his mother there is a gap of three
to four weeks. At first the embryo clings tenuously to the
wall of the uterus becoming more firmly fixed through the
placenta and umbilical cord. During this time the baby is

developing a spinal cord, a little heart and a digestive system. The tiny embryo is being 'made in the secret place' (Ps.139:15) and waits in silence for a verdict on his presence. Will his existence be received with joy or anger? Will he be accepted or rejected by the most important person in his life? What feelings will form the emotional environment in which he is going to live for the next eight months? Will there be the positive feelings of love, joy, happiness or the negative ones of anxiety, resentment, depression and fear?

Dr Frank Lake and Dr Thomas Verney 'believe that in some mysterious way, the human embryo can remember and feel, even at the earliest stages of life.'[1] Certainly once the foetus is connected to the mother's blood supply through the placenta and umbilical cord it is in direct contact with whatever is happening to the mother. It is therefore not difficult to understand that as well as receiving nourishment, the baby will also be receiving the full range of all the mother's emotions. 'This intimate connection of mother and foetus is not so surprising,' writes Dr Frank Lake. 'When we are angry or terrified, every cell in our bodies is informed of the emotional emergency. From the tips of the toes that curl up in tension to the hair that "stands on end", we show and can recognise the signs and symptoms of these strong emotions. Why should this communication exclude the womb?'[2]

I find Dr Lake's proposed emotional connection between mother and baby easy to believe. First because of the physical reaction many people have to the sight of another's pain. Just seeing an accident can cause a shooting pain to pierce the whole physical body of a witness. It seems as if every cell responds to the picture the brain is receiving when a sudden release of adrenalin rushes through the body's system. Normally we are ignorant of the messages our body cells are receiving unless, as in shock, the signal is amplified. But our cells, in fact, are constant receptors of signals and the baby in the womb is part of his mother's system and will, likewise, be receiving all these messages.

Secondly, it is easy to believe because of my experience in the counselling room and occasionally in larger meetings. My colleague and I have ministered to people who have regressed into the womb, sovereignly through the Holy Spirit, and have re-experienced a variety of repressed feelings. In some instances great discomfort has been localised in the middle of the stomach and the counsellee will tear at an imaginary umbilical cord, trying to escape the influx of bad feelings he senses coming into him.

Summarising his findings from over 1,200 subjects Dr Lake identifies a 'Maternal Foetal Distress Syndrome': 'the emotional state of the pregnant mother is transmitted to the foetus. Her joy and recognition of her changed state leads to foetal joy in being recognized, accepted and, indeed, welcomed. Her distress, if that is her condition during the first trimester, invades the foetus in the form of a bitter, black flood.'[3]

Mother's task during pregnancy

Recognition and welcome

With all this in mind it would seem that the first natural and normal response of the mother should be one of recognition and welcome. She begins by suspecting that she is pregnant. As the days pass she becomes more sure of baby's existence within her. Finally, with a visit to the doctor comes the moment of full recognition. The quality of that first acknowledgement and subsequent welcome creates a foundation that could affect the baby's attitude in all future encounters and relationships.

Lucy is a friend of mine who seems to live in a frenetic whirl of activity. She is the life and soul of every party. She rushes about helping and rescuing one friend after another.

Her life has appeared to be dominated by a need to be acceptable to everyone. Each July this activity seems to become more compulsive and on one occasion even led to a near break-down. Recently during a time of prayer with another friend Lucy was asked when she was born. As she was born in December this seemed irrelevant to her problem. However, during the following week this question started her on an amazing train of thought. She had been conceived in the spring by her mother having an extra-marital affair. Her husband was away during this time and came home in July when the mother was nearly four months pregnant. He gave her an ultimatum. It was either the baby or him. The mother was forced to give up the child for adoption. My friend then began to realise the implication of these facts. It was during a crucial time in the womb that she had been rejected instead of welcomed and this had laid a foundation which had governed her thinking and behaviour all her life. This insight led to a feeling of relief. At last she felt she was dealing with a concrete problem instead of irrational behaviour over which she had no control.

Recognition and welcome, particularly by those we are closely connected with, are vital in helping us to achieve a healthy view of ourselves. Throughout our lives an enthusiastic welcome will often do us more good than a visit to the doctor. Our small grandsons have not yet learned the British art of hiding their feelings! When we visit them they express, openly and spontaneously, exactly how they feel. They come rushing out of the house, arms outstretched, their upturned faces glowing in the anticipation of an afternoon of cuddles and attention from their adoring grandparents. We may have had a difficult journey, it may be a grey day, we may have left behind some awkward unsolved problems, but in that moment of glorious welcome all is forgotten. It is as if the sun has come out and all is well with the world.

Feeling welcomed, then, is important for our well-being. The first ever experience of that maternal welcome may be foundational to the way the child will subsequently come to view life.

The perfect hostess

If the initial task of the mother is to give the baby full recognition and welcome the next task should follow on naturally. It is that of becoming a good hostess for this amazing little guest. Her attention must be concentrated on the physical, emotional and spiritual well-being of her baby. Her womb is to be his home for the next eight months. As he grows physically during that time so does his sense of awareness. By six months he can hear and respond. By this time the mother needs to become more overt and definite in her recognition of the baby's presence. Time spent massaging and talking to the baby will increase his sense of well-being and of confidence in a good maternal presence.

My youngest daughter, Tasha, is, at the moment of writing, six months pregnant. She recently met up with her older sister Debby, after a gap of a few months. They were chatting together in my kitchen when Debby suddenly put her hands on Tasha's tummy and said, 'Now I must get to know the baby.' She then proceeded to massage Tasha's bump and talk to it gently and quietly.

Bonding

Dr Verney tells the sad story of Kristina, a robust newborn baby girl, who refused her mother's breast from birth. At first the gynaecologist thought the baby must be ill but when she devoured a bottle of formula milk he decided it was a temporary reaction. However, the next day Kristina's reaction to her mother's breast was exactly the same and she continued to turn her face away. The doctor decided to conduct an experiment. He placed the baby at another woman's breast and to his astonishment the baby grasped it and sucked for all she was worth. Returning to the baby's real mother he asked her questions about her pregnancy. It transpired that she had not wanted to get pregnant and when she found she was, wished for an abortion. 'My husband wanted the child. That's why I had her,' she told the doctor. As Dr Verney explained, Kristina 'had been painfully aware of her mother's rejection for a long time. She refused to bond with her mother after birth because her mother had refused to bond with her before it. Kristina had been shut out emotionally in the womb and now, though barely four days old, she was determined to protect herself from her mother in any way she could.'[4]

The last three months of pregnancy are important months for both mother and child. The bonding between the baby and her mother should start in the womb and as we have seen in the case of Kristina a baby will not bond to an unwelcoming mother. The mother must lead the way in the bonding process. The baby cannot bond alone. 'If his mother shuts down emotionally he is at a loss,' says Dr Verney.[5]

Once the six-month period is reached the baby has become an emotionally feeling little person. 'A foetus who can see, hear, experience, taste and, on a primitive level, even learn in utero.'[6] Therefore, the mother should be giving special attention during these last months to the person within her. 'His demands are not unreasonable: all he wants is some love and attention and, when he gets them, everything else, including bonding, follows naturally.'[7]

So the mother's main concern during the nine months will be first to make the baby within her feel welcome, to initiate the bonding process, then to nurture it and provide, as much as possible, a secure, peaceful haven where the baby may achieve his main task of growing.

The baby's task

Baby's major objective is to receive nurture and to grow in basic trust. A harmonious, tranquil environment will enable the baby to take in an adequate amount of nourishment. It is the start of a long period of total reliance. The baby can do nothing to help himself in this. His life depends on another. The achievement of comfortable and trusting dependence at this stage will mean that in later years the growing teenager or adult will be free from painful dependence on others or abnormal detachment from others. However, if he spends his months in the womb defending himself against the invasion of bad feelings from the mother, or loud angry noises around him, he will not achieve these important pre-natal tasks. Instead he will find another foundation being laid down at the roots of his personality. He will have learned to attach with pain and receive with discomfort. Basic trust will become unnatural for him.

If the mother's task is primarily one of provision and the baby's one of receiving what she provides, where does this leave the father? Once that initial task of impregnation has been achieved should he step aside and leave the mother to work at producing a healthy baby?

The task of the father

'Being confident of this that he who began a good work in you will carry it on to completion until the day of Christ Jesus' (Phil.1:6).

When God initiates the new birth in someone he doesn't then withdraw and have nothing more to do with that person. He cares for what He has begun. God is our Heavenly Father and exemplifies loving parenthood. As we shall see in the following chapters, both the feminine and the masculine aspects of parenting are involved in the care God gives us. However, though God's mothering is discernible in the Bible, it is the concept of His Fatherhood that dominates.

As we follow His relationship with His people from creation to the birth of the early church we are struck by His constant involvement in their lives. Frequently this is strongly masculine as He initiates first the creation of the world, then the choosing of His people, the setting aside of Prophets, Priests and Kings, the sending of His Son and the empowering of His church. We see Him initiating, guiding, protecting, disciplining, supporting and empowering, all of which are the more masculine tasks which pertain to the father. These activities in no way preclude God from also adopting the more feminine role of giving nurture and loving care to His children. Certainly no earthly father should be excluded from the more feminine nurturing tasks either.

Protecting and supporting

However, it is the husband who initiates the sexual act of love and penetrates his wife. It is one of the millions of his spermatozoa which will reach her ovum to conceive a new life. The father's task for the next nine months is not to withdraw to the side lines as a passive onlooker. Just as God continued to be actively involved with His own creation so must the human father maintain such active involvement as is suited to his male identity − that of protector and supporter. His job is to provide the right environment for his wife to nurture the baby within her. She needs to be encouraged and supported in this by her husband, who will stand like a watchman between his embryonic family and the surrounding community. He should be protecting the home base from any intrusions which might threaten to disturb the peace within the family boundary. A wonderful miracle of creation is taking place in the mother-to-be and father should adopt a protective stance enabling the gestation process to take place in the best possible circumstances.

Bonding

Far from being a supernumerary in this drama, the father plays a vital role throughout the pregnancy. His wife needs him to be there; so too does the baby. The tiny creature needs to grow accustomed to Daddy's voice and touch as well. He needs to have the father's recognition and welcome. When our daughter Charlotte and her husband Chris were expecting their first child Chris used to sit beside Charlotte in the evening and put his hand on the side of her tummy and talk to the baby. As the days went by they noticed that whenever Chris did this the baby would move over in the womb and nestle close to his father's hand.

Francis MacNutt, a late parent himself, describes the father's role with evident personal delight: 'Until I began studying about the unborn child, I did not realise that, next to the mother's love for her child, the father's love for his wife and the child-to-be is the most important factor influencing the child's future happiness.'[8]

A happy, harmonious marriage is the best environment for a baby both inside and outside the womb. God's ideal for marriage is oneness. 'For this reason a man will leave his father and mother and be united to his wife, and they will become one flesh' (Gen.2:24). Man and woman procreated the baby together and together they must provide the nurturing ambience in which the baby can grow until it is ready to be born.

Unfortunately we have long since been shut out of paradise and the perfect has been lost to us. Though much

of the pain and danger has now been eliminated from childbearing through the advances of science, we nevertheless still
have to live in a fallen world from which none can be totally
protected. .

The traumas of pregnancy

As a mother

Perhaps some women reading this chapter have been
reminded of their own experience of pregnancy. My first
baby was born six weeks prematurely after weeks of illness
and anxiety. No one was really to blame, though my
ignorance and immaturity and a busy doctor's oversight did
nothing to help.

In the counselling room we are frequently called upon to
minister to women who have experienced unavoidable
problems during pregnancy. Perhaps your pregnancy was
unexpected or possibly unwelcome. Maybe resentment and
bitterness as well as sickness were a part of those early weeks.
Marriage is not a bed of roses for everyone and maybe you
experienced nine months of fear and anxiety. Abuse and
violence have sometimes haunted both the mother and the
unborn child. Worry over money, housing or the husband's
work, may have clouded those months for others.

If you are still looking back on your pregnancy with
sadness, pain or guilt instead of joy and pleasure, maybe you
should find a quiet place alone (or with a friend) and ask God
to heal you. The suggestions at the end of this chapter may
help you enter into the healing God has in store for you.

As a baby

More frequently we are involved in praying for those whose
early beginnings have affected them in some way. Even if this

is not obviously the root of their problem we have found that to pray through the time in the womb has had a releasing and cleansing effect for many people.

I remember once praying for a depressed lady. We had ministered to her periodically over several months and her root problem obviously lay in a later stage of development. However, on this occasion I felt God prompt me to go back to her time in the womb and pray through those months with her. Nothing very dramatic happened during the prayer but when I had finished she remained very still for a long time. She then raised her head and with tears in her eyes said to us, 'I feel so happy.'

As we have seen 'any severe maternal distress, whatever its cause, imprints itself on the foetus.'[9]. This distress can launch one on a lifetime of mistrust and an inability to receive good from others or to feel good about oneself. If you struggle to any degree with these problems or if you know of particular anxieties or difficulties surrounding your mother whilst she was still carrying you in the womb, you may like to use the following prayers and exercises. For some it is sufficient to be alone with God and allow Him to minister to your heart. Others will need the support and presence of a friend or counsellor. Certainly if you suspect that some such primal affliction has caused major difficulties in your own life you will need a 'safe place' created for you before you can risk descending into the abyss in the process of healing.

Exercises

For Mothers
Was your pregnancy clouded by illness or bad feelings?
If so find a quiet spot either alone or with your friend/counsellor.

1. Begin by inviting God's presence to be with you. Ask for

His protection around you.

2. Starting from the first moment you suspected you were pregnant describe your feelings and reactions aloud to God.

3. As the feelings begin to surface give yourself permission to express them fully.

4. Once the feelings are out in the open, begin to forgive anyone you perceive as having caused you pain or difficulty during the pregnancy. Also ask God to forgive you for any wrong you committed, against the baby or anyone else.

5. Ask Jesus to heal the emotional wounds left from the trauma. Give Him time to do this in whatever way He wishes.

6. Pray about the possibility of talking to your child about his beginnings and asking forgiveness for any hurt you may have unwittingly inflicted on him.

7. In the coming days and weeks continue to open your heart to God's healing love.

For the Baby
1. Do you currently experience difficulty in:
   Trusting your environment and those around you?
   Receiving love and affection?
   Feeling acceptable to others?
   Relating intimately with those near to you?
   Feeling guilty for no obvious reason?
   Calling on someone without a specific invitation?

2. Write down in your diary what you know of the circumstances of your conception and the nine months in the womb. Were you wanted, planned for, welcomed? Was your mother happy and well while you were in the womb? Was she supported by your father?

3. Using the knowledge you have gained from 1. and 2. with

your friend/counsellor pray through the nine months in the womb. Give plenty of time for any feelings to surface and be expressed.

OR if you do not have any clear facts to work with pray slowly through the nine months asking the Holy Spirit to surface anything He knows to be in need of healing.

4. Another exercise you may like to try is to take an imaginary journey to the 'secret place' (Ps.139:15).

On our many journeys abroad I use the following prayer, especially at the time when the plane takes off.

'Christ be with me, Christ within me,
Christ behind me, Christ before me,
Christ beside me, Christ to win me,
Christ to comfort and restore me,
Christ beneath me, Christ above me,
Christ in quiet, Christ in danger,
Christ in hearts of all that love me,
Christ in mouth of friend and stranger.'
(St Patrick's Breastplate. C.F. Alexander's translation)

You are about to make a journey so start by repeating St Patrick's prayer slowly, acknowledging the truth of Christ's presence with you on the way.

The Journey (led by your friend/counsellor)
Imagine yourself swimming in clear water.
Dip beneath the surface of the water.
Swim down towards a secret, submerged cave.
Enter the cave.
Look around. What do you see?
Take time to notice the walls and the shape of the cave.
Notice how your body feels. Is there pain or discomfort anywhere?
What are your emotions? Are you fearful, anxious, angry, happy, peaceful, sad?

Stay with the feelings and allow them to grow.
Experiment by expressing the feelings with a noise.
Notice there is no exit to the cave.
How does that make you feel?
Now there are noises outside the cave.
Allow yourself to react to these noises.
Seek the awareness of God's presence with you in the cave.
'Where can I go from your Spirit?
Where can I flee from your presence?
If I go up to the Heavens, you are there;
If I make my bed in the depths, you are there' (Ps.139:7,8).
Jesus is in there with you by His Spirit.
Draw close to his welcoming and protective presence.
Share the feelings you are experiencing with Him.
Draw all the bad feelings out of yourself and give them to
Him.
Let Him give you something in return.

5. In your journal write down the feelings you have just
experienced, any new insights gained or healing received.
Are you aware of any attitudes of heart, which were formed
at that time, which you now know are ungodly and need
changing? Renounce them and ask God to forgive you and
help you form new ones.

6. Spend some time releasing forgiveness to anyone
(including of course your mother if that is the case) who
may have caused you pain during the nine months in the
womb.

7. Spend time in the coming days and weeks meditating on
God's Word:

> For you created my inmost being: you knit me together
> in my mother's womb. I praise you because I am fearfully
> and wonderfully made; your works are wonderful, I know
> that full well. My frame was not hidden from you when

I was made in the secret place. When I was woven together in the depths of the earth, your eyes saw my unformed body. All the days ordained for me are written in your book before one of them came to be (Ps.139:13,14,15,16).

Come into God's presence and become aware of His eyes upon you. Look for the recognition and welcome in His eyes for you.

When Jesus saw Nathanael approaching, he said of him,
'Here is a true Israelite, in whom there is nothing false.'
'How do you know me?' Nathanael asked.
Jesus answered, 'I saw you while you were still under the fig-tree before Philip called you.'
Then Nathanael declared, 'Rabbi, you are the Son of God; you are the King of Israel' (Jn.1:47—49).

Take Nathanael's place and see yourself walking towards Jesus. See the recognition in the eyes of Jesus. Hear His welcome for you.

4. A HAZARDOUS JOURNEY
(Birth)

'To the woman he said, "I will greatly increase your pains in childbearing; with pain you will give birth to children" ' (Gen.3:16).

'A woman giving birth to a child has pain because her time has come; but when her baby is born she forgets the anguish because of her joy that a child is born into the world' (Jn.16:21).

For a woman to give birth to a seven- or eight-pound baby is extremely hard work! It can be a tiring experience too for the father especially if he is present at the birth. For the baby, however, the experience may also be traumatic. Dr Frank Lake describes the sometimes catastrophic process with feeling. 'So although for most people the process of birth may be tough but tolerable, for some it can be devastating in its destructiveness. Cataclysmic muscular convulsions turn a peaceful haven into a crushing hell. This "no-exit" phase, before the cervix begins to open, can last for some hours. The next phase of travel through the pelvis is at best an energetic struggle, at worst a brain-destroying, suffocating, twisting, tearing, crushing torture, in which the will to live may be extinguished and a longing to die take its place. The hazards of obstruction, impaction, prolonged delays due to uterine inertia, or sudden violent extrusion when induction puts the uterine muscle in spasm, the hazards of forceps delivery, abnormal presentations, asphyxia as a result of the cord being round the neck, breech births or emergency Caesarean sections, all these possibilities of profound discouragement and catastrophe may occur during this phase.'[1] Not every birth is so traumatic and for those for whom it is, many are reasonably healed through the subsequent loving care and security of parents.

Labour for the mother

The labour then is just what the word describes — hard work. The mother's job is one of co-operation with her own body and with the medical staff. The more calm she can maintain, the more she is able to relax and practise her breathing techniques, the easier and quicker the process will be. Fear and anxiety increase muscle tension which in turn adds to the mother's discomfort and prolongs the baby's journey into the world. In the early stages of labour before the totally absorbing work of pushing begins, the mother, as well as co-operating with the contractions, should also be encouraging and calming her baby. Francis and Judith MacNutt in their book *Praying for your Unborn Child* make a helpful observation. 'During the process of labour and delivery, mother and father should continue to be present to the child and guide it gently through the birth canal. Through this continued loving presence of the parents to the child the labour pains are continually reduced and the delivery becomes that much easier.'[2]

Labour for the father

The task of giving birth belongs to two people: the mother and baby. Father can help, medical staff can help but only the mother can push the baby into the world and only the baby can keep a strong grasp on life and maintain the struggle to be born. However, the father's presence is important to both mother and baby at this time. He is inextricably and intimately involved with the process. 'I couldn't have done it without him,' is the comment of many mothers after delivery is over. For my two births in England David was present throughout the labour and delivery but for the two South American ones he was excluded from the actual delivery in case, like many South American fathers, he should faint or get too excited! I missed his comforting and reassuring presence.

While his wife works so hard the father-to-be should be giving her continual support both emotionally and physically. His job is one of encouragement and reassurance to both mother and the baby. By the end of nine months the baby should know Daddy's voice and touch and will benefit from his calming influence. Before the birth and during it a baby should have the wonderful security of a strong masculine presence in his life. God 'created man in his own image, in the image of God he created him; male and female he created them' (Gen.1:27). The male and female together provide the perfect environment for a baby. The strong protection and the consistent nurture, the tender care and the loving discipline should all be present. Through his parents a baby will receive his first impressions of God. A good relationship to God later in life often hinges on these early experiences with parents and especially with the father.

During the last stages of labour the father is more physically involved, supporting his wife and helping her continue the breathing techniques. His presence will be an encouragement to her and when the baby is finally born it should be the father's privilege to hand their baby over to his wife. Then together they can experience the joy of continuing to bond with the baby they have been getting to know over the past months.

The baby's labour

'How he is born — whether it is painful or easy, smooth or violent — largely determines who he becomes and how he will view the world around him. Whether he is five, ten, forty or seventy, a part of him always looks out at the world through the eyes of the newly born child he once was. That is why Freud called the pleasure and pain that accompany birth "primal emotions". None of us ever entirely escapes their pull.'[3]

For some babies the labour is prolonged and the delay can cause extreme discomfort. One woman experienced anger towards her mother all her life and only after reliving her birth was she able to understand her anger and forgive her mother for causing her to be stuck in the birth canal for an unbearable length of time. Witnessing a young man re-experience his birth on one occasion I felt exhausted by the end just watching the effort he had to make as he frantically struggled to come out of that restricted place.

The baby's desire for life must be strong enough to push through the barriers and fight to enter the frightening unknown of life outside the womb. He needs the full support and co-operation of mother (and father if possible) to achieve his task without suffering unbearable consequences which could leave him with repressed fears and pain, causing him various difficulties later — claustrophobia, agoraphobia, fear of separation, abnormal anxiety and panic attacks. For nine months baby has been alone with mother, listening to her every heart beat and digestive gurgling. He has moved with her, rested with her, heard her speak, sing, sigh and cry. He has been part of her emotionally and physically and then in a number of hours he has separated from her, taken his first breath, experienced space, weight, heat, cold, strong but unfamiliar hands, loud noises and bright lights. All this is traumatic enough to the baby but quite possibly, to top it all, he was almost immediately put into a cot and wheeled away from mother and left to cry piteously alone in an unfamiliar world.

Many of those we counsel suffer from separation anxiety. Some of these damaged personalities experience a type of hysterical reaction that dreads being left alone and craves attention and company. Yet others have somehow split from the pain of needing someone and have adopted a protective role of non-relatedness. The terror of ever needing anyone again is greater than never having someone there when needed. As Dr Charles Whitfield points out: 'Fear of abandonment goes all the way back to our earliest seconds, minutes and hours of existence. Related to the issue of trust and distrust, it is often exaggerated among children who grew up in troubled or dysfunctional families. Thus, to counter this fear, we often mistrust; we shut out our feelings so we don't feel the hurt.'[4]

One young woman suffering from a severe separation anxiety said that her mother (following advice which was fashionable at the time) used to shut her away in a nursery to scream alone for hours. To be left or to have to leave people now, twenty years later, causes her extreme feelings of panic. 'The newborn may be left alone long enough to be nudged to the edge of the abyss of non-being, trembling through the phase of separation-anxiety, eventually to fall in a moment of horror, over the edge into nothingness, into the abandonment of hope, love, desire for life and expectation of access to humanity . . . It is from these experiences that our perception of the cosmos derives. Our basic expectations of what it means to live outside in "God's world", and to depend on others for gentle handling, love and mercy, take their origin here.'[5]

Today in most maternity wards around the world it is well understood that what the baby most needs is to be laid on the mother's breast immediately after birth. Then he can still hear her familiar voice and heart beat and continue to be sustained and nurtured by her but this time through the breast and not the umbilical cord. Recovering from the birth experience in this way will heal the pain and anxiety any prolonged and difficult birth may have caused. The mother may herself be exhausted but this recovery time with the baby will become a labour of joy. Most mothers welcome this time with the baby. In fact her instinct tells her it is right and needful and contributes to a mother's recovery.

When our grandson Andrew was born he was very wakeful at first and cried every hour during the night. Eventually our daughter Tasha became so exhausted she took him into her bed, whereupon he immediately settled down and slept for four or five hours at a stretch. For the early weeks of his life he spent every night in his mother's bed and so long as he was tucked up against her side he slept peacefully. He eventually made the separation into his own cot, but not until he was ready.

The birth trauma and present-day problems

Some would question the assumption that a difficult and prolonged birth could still exert an influence upon a person, twenty years after the event. Dr Lake is convinced, however, that peri-natal injuries do lie at the root of certain personality disorders and irrational fears. Other psychiatrists are also quoted by Dr Lake as holding this view. Among them is D.W. Winnicott, one of the most highly regarded British pediatricians and psychoanalysts. He held the same views about birth and the relevance of birth traumas. 'Psychiatrists who value his work in all other respects tend to overlook his papers on birth trauma.'[6]

Along with modern technology there has been a sharp rise in the number of Caesarean sections. Dr Verney has noticed one long-term effect among his patients of being born in this way; an intense craving for physical contact. 'This is probably because the Caesarean's delivery deprives him of the sensual moments that a vaginally delivered baby has during birth − both excruciating pain and the extreme pleasure. These sensual feelings are the forerunners of adult sexuality, and the surgically delivered person may never quite overcome their loss.'[7]

A breech birth may also leave a person with some long-term effect, as may umbilical cord difficulties. A baby born with the cord around his neck may suffer from throat or speech difficulties later.[8] The premature baby, born before his time, or the sick baby whose life hangs in the balance, will not only have to fight for survival but often suffer the insecurity of being taken away from maternal comfort and put alone in a sick baby unit. As I have already noted, more hospitals today are growing wise to the great need a newborn baby has for his mother's touch and the sound of her voice and the mother, if fit enough, is allowed to help in the care of her baby.

For most people the experience of being born is beyond the reach of their conscious memory. Recent studies, however, indicate that some can recall the events surrounding their birth. These studies provide the evidence that a baby's mind is recording his birth. Dr Verney illustrates this with the story of Ricky Burke. At six years old Ricky was tormented by horrible nightmares. Night after night, just after falling asleep, he would begin to throw himself around and curse in a vocabulary far beyond the power of a child his age. Sometimes he would also speak in a different language. After listening to a broadcast about dreams expressing birth memories, his mother started thinking about Ricky's birth. She had had a very bad labour and the baby had been born nearly dead. The overtired doctor had cursed as he delivered the baby, then a priest had been called out to administer last rites to Ricky. 'Ricky's nightmare grew out of his birth memory; his swear words were those he had heard the doctors using; his language, the priest's Latin.'[9]

Children between the ages of two and three are most able to recall their births. After three or four, these memories seem to fade permanently from consciousness. Judith and Francis MacNutt recount their daughter's experience: 'When our little girl, Rachel, was three years old, I asked her if she remembered her birth. She had several memories which indicated some recall. Her first response was: it felt like swimming. When questioned further, she said it also felt like exercise, and she became very tired. She also remembered a bright light. Now that Rachel is five, I have questioned her again, but she can't remember any details of her birth.' [10]

The memory of one's birth may be beyond one's reach but nothing is beyond the reach of God. Just as the power of the cross spans all time and its salvation, through faith, is for all people from the beginning to the end of time, so its healing power can touch every moment of our lives from the moment of conception to the present day.

'Fear not, for I have redeemed you; I have called you by name; you are mine. When you pass through the waters, I will be with you; and when you pass through the rivers, they will not sweep over you' (Is.43:1,2).

Exercises

1. Write in your journal all you know about your birth.
Were you a full-term baby?
Were there any complications?
What were the complications, if any?
Were you born quickly or was it a long birth?
Were you born in hospital or at home?
Were you separated from your mother at birth?
Was your father present at your birth?

2. Go back in your imagination to that secret cave under the sea.

Once more become aware of the presence of Jesus with you.
Spend time recapturing the feeling of His presence.
Now notice how constricted the cave has become.
Feel the discomfort.
Accept the need to leave your cave.
Notice how you feel about that.
'When you pass through the waters I will be with you!'
Let Jesus lead you through the waters of your birth into Life
outside the womb.
Go slowly and be aware of any sensations or feelings you
may be having on this journey.

3. In your journal write a description of your journey.

4. Write down any present-day problems or difficulties you
think may relate to your birth.
Do you suffer from claustrophobia?
Do you often feel angry without good reason?
Do you feel continually frustrated or obstructed in the things
you want to do?
Have you any speech difficulties or recurring throat
problems?
Are you afraid of being left alone or being separated from
those you love?
Do you feel you rush through life always in a hurry?
Is yours a lazy mind that finds concentration difficult?

5. Share your findings with your friend/counsellor.
Pray together and allow God time to minister His healing
to one specific problem. Deal with that before moving on
to the next.

6. Remember that feeling pain and grieving loss has a
cleansing effect.

7. Releasing forgiveness to those who have caused you to
be hurt helps release your own inbuilt healing processes and
will bring closure to the wound.

8. Spend time meditating on God's Word such as the verses already quoted:

'Fear not, for I have redeemed you; I have called you by name; you are mine. When you pass through the waters, I will be with you; and when you pass through the rivers, they will not sweep over you. When you walk through the fire, you will not be burned; the flames will not set you ablaze. For I am the Lord, your God, the Holy One of Israel, your Saviour' (Is.43:1,2,3).

Meditate on the experiences of Jesus on the Cross, the physical suffering, the emotional suffering, the spiritual suffering. Remember His cry of deep anguish. 'My God, my God, why have you forsaken me?' (Mark 15:34) At that moment He knew the pain of separation from His Father and complete aloneness. You can take your loneliness and your fear of separation to Him because 'by His wounds we are healed' (Is.53:5).

Visualise Him on the cross and take the suffering of your birth to Him. Deliberately unburden those sufferings on to Him.

'The eternal God is your refuge, and underneath are the everlasting arms' (Deut.33:27).

Imagine yourself as a baby nestling in God's arms. In His arms you will find the nurture of a mother and the protection of a father.

5. 'HIS MAJESTY, THE BABY'
(First stage, 0−12 months)

> 'It is not so much that the infant thinks he is the world, that he desires to be omnipotent and omnipresent, but rather that there is no reason to be aware that there is anything else, anything other than self, until the "not-self" makes its presence felt.' Robin Skynner[1]

The needs of the baby

A baby is born totally dependent upon others. He can do nothing for himself. He has only one way of drawing attention to his needs and that is by crying. He cannot verbalise them; he cannot make Mummy notice by tugging at her skirts. Unable to deliver any appropriate signals other than crying he is reliant on someone being present to respond sensitively to his many requirements. He is thrust into the world without the capacity to care for himself or articulate any specific need. He expects his needs to be met as if by right.

Nurture

The most basic and urgent need of the newborn baby is nurture. Without an adequate supply of milk the baby will die and so most of his crying will be to this end. For nine months the baby has been receiving nurture effortlessly from mother through the umbilical cord. If at all possible he needs to continue to be attached to her for his food, not through the umbilical cord as before but through the breast for whose nurture, though totally available to him, he now has to make some effort.

In our western society breast-feeding is not generally considered a convenient or popular form of feeding, since it ties the mother to the baby for many months. But as we shall see this is exactly what God intended to be the most beneficial for the baby. It is important to point out at this stage that some mothers earnestly desire to breast-feed and for good reasons have found it impossible. As Dr Verney says, 'What really counts psychologically is what emotions are communicated to the infant during feeding. A child can feel loved whether he is breast- or bottle-fed.'[2] The emotional needs of the baby can still be met through bottle-feeding if the following points are taken into account.

Sucking

Sucking is good exercise for the baby. It also meets an acute need; a need which is put there to ensure survival. Nevertheless many mothers do not always appreciate how strong that need is. The biological need to suck can be urgent in the new baby. Bottle-fed babies are too often left with this need for 'perioral stimulation' (around the mouth) inadequately met. Not only is the bottle more quickly emptied but the traditional rubber teat does not provide the same stimulation as the mother's nipple. The need for sucking may be quite independent of hunger. 'It is largely satisfied through nursing, especially in the breast-fed infant who has to work hard for his meal, but a large number of babies are left, even after feeding, with still unsatisfied sucking needs and this is experienced as an unbearable tension in the mouth.'³

Providing there is an adequate supply of breast-milk and the mother's nipple is able to stand up to the pressing demands of a hungry baby, breast-feeding is preferable in every way to the bottle. It provides immunity because the colostrum secreted by the mother in the early days is rich in anti-bodies. The great benefits of breast-feeding have been documented by Montagu in his book *Touching*. He draws the reader's attention to a pilot study done on 173 children followed from birth to ten years old, including both breast-fed babies and bottle-fed babies. This study found that the infants who had not been breast-fed had 'four times as many respiratory infections, twenty times more diarrhoea, twenty-two more miscellaneous infections, eight times as much eczema, twenty-one times more asthma and twenty-seven times more hay fever.'⁴

Bonding

Besides these purely physical benefits breast-feeding is also crucial because it provides the opportunity for mother and baby to bond. The baby is attached physically to mother through the mouth and at the same time the baby's hand is able to knead and feel the breast gently. The baby is being held close to the mother for long periods and probably at more frequent intervals than a bottle-fed baby. Too frequently the bottle has been regarded as an easy option; a time-saving method of feeding. It is tempting for mother to stick a bottle into the baby's mouth, prop it up with a pillow and dash off to do the household chores. The milk used for bottle-feeding is often more filling and so the baby will last longer between feeds and possibly go through the night at an earlier age, all of which enables and encourages the mother to return to her normal separate existence more quickly. Unfortunately by doing this the baby is robbed, both physically and emotionally, of the basic requirement of bonding to a constant, reliable, familiar mother-figure. However, a bottle-fed baby will not suffer any emotional deprivation, providing his mother is prepared to spend just as much time with him as she would if he were breast-fed.

According to a study by Burton Jones, the composition of milk in the various species relates to their different feeding schedules. The less they feed their young the higher is the protein and fat content. For example, rabbits and hares feed every twenty-four hours and the tree shrew every forty-eight hours. These animals have milk with a very high fat content. On the other hand apes and humans have milk with a very low fat content which means they need to feed their young at frequent intervals. This indicates, 'that the human mother, like the ape mother, is designed to carry her baby with her wherever she goes.'[5]

The bonding or connection between a mother and baby is more than just a physical and emotional one. It is sometimes quite uncanny how a mother will know when there is something wrong with her baby, even though it is not obvious to anyone else. This unusual bonding of baby with mother was demonstrated by the Russians, experimenting for military purposes with a newborn litter of rabbits. They were placed aboard a submerged submarine. 'The mother was kept at home base in a laboratory with electrodes implanted in her brain. Periodically one of the baby rabbits aboard the sub was killed, and at that moment the fact was recorded in the laboratory by an abrupt change in the brain waves of the mother. Telepathic communication to a living creature was able to get through from the bottom of the ocean where no physical method that we know of could reach back to land.'[6]

Pleasure

After breast-feeding four children and watching six grandchildren being breast-fed, I am convinced a baby experiences enormous pleasure at the breast. It would seem to be recorded somewhere in baby's brain as a time of blissful oneness with the source of life. Many children continue thumb-sucking long after the bottle or breast has been discontinued and the need for sucking passed. Usually the habit is indulged in at times of stress or tiredness, as if the child is unconsciously desiring to return to a particularly pleasant experience of babyhood, calling up feelings of peace and relaxation.

Montagu relates the case of a two-and-a-half-year-old child referred by a dermatologist for psychiatric study because of hair loss. The child frequently cuddled herself in her mother's arms and sucked milk from a bottle and while doing this she would pull out her own hair and brush the strands across her nose as she sucked the bottle. On investigation the doctor discovered that the habit had begun a year earlier at the start of a punitive programme of toilet training which put the child under considerable stress. At this point the child refused solid food and would only drink from a bottle, pulling at her hair and tickling her nose at the same time. Further questioning revealed that the child had been breast-fed for two weeks only and then abruptly weaned as the mother feared she had insufficient milk. However, the most remarkable fact was that on examination the mother was discovered to have a circle of coarse hair around her nipples which would have tickled the baby's nose as she suckled during those first two weeks of life. In order to test this out a teat was constructed with a ring of coarse human hair around its base. As the child sucked at the teat she slowly turned the bottle brushing the hairs against her nose and upper lip. From that time on the child stopped pulling out her hair. Under stress this child had regressed to a time, recorded in her memory, as being happy and relaxed.

By God's design breast-feeding meets so many of the basic needs of the first stage of development. These range through the physical needs for a perfect food, protection from infection and adequate sucking time, to the emotional needs for pleasure and bonding to one constant care-giver who is on hand twenty-four hours a day.

Omnipotence

For many this seems a strange and incomprehensible need for a baby to have. Many people hold to an irrational belief that it spoils a baby to pick him up and cuddle him too much. Studies in child-rearing are now showing us the opposite. In fact, it would seem that a short period of feeling omnipotent is necessary for the baby; a time when he is the centre of mother's attention and when his needs are immediately met.

'The infant is necessarily "all", "everything", indeed "God", until it discovers otherwise.'[7] And he will find in good time that he is not really omnipotent and that the world does not really revolve around him, as he thought. But for the first six months the baby is not emotionally equipped to cope with aloneness, frustration or pain. It is not possible to 'spoil' a baby by giving him too much attention at this stage; only to spoil him by giving him insufficient attention. Mary Salter Ainsworth's studies show that:

An infant whose mother is sensitive, accessible, and responsive to him, who accepts his behaviour and is cooperative in dealing with him, is far from being the demanding and unhappy child that some theories might suggest. Instead, mothering of this sort is evidently compatible with a child who is developing a limited measure of self-reliance by the time of his first birthday combined with a high degree of trust in his mother and enjoyment of her company.[8]

The task of the mother and father

The task of the mother then is to be there physically and emotionally for her baby. The mother's reliable, consistent presence and succour at this time are the main requirements, 'so that the infant can internalise steadily the physical and psychic nourishment she provides.'[9]

The task of the father in the first months is to guard the boundaries, keeping the coast clear for this nurturing to take place with optimal peace and quiet. For me to give enough time to the new baby my husband David would take over, as much as was possible, caring for the other children. In fact for the first few months I slept in the spare room with the new baby, while he dealt with the nocturnal needs of the others. This gave me the opportunity for some extra sleep as well as a peaceful time alone with the baby and I remember those exclusive night feeds as very special times of bonding with the new baby.

It is important for mother and baby that these times are made possible by the father.

When a child is born, the mother needs temporarily to enter into an intense and exclusive relationship with it, regressing to a state of what Winnicott has termed 'primary maternal preoccupation' in order to perceive the infant's needs directly through re-experiencing that stage herself. The father, if sufficiently mature, is prepared to forgo his previous unfettered enjoyment of his spouse to allow her to carry out the maternal function while he fulfils his responsibility by 'holding the life line' and supporting the mother in her biological task.[10]

The task of the baby

Many professional therapists and child psychologists have

mapped out different developmental models. Erikson's model is particularly useful. He suggests that each stage brings with it a special developmental task, sometimes accomplished well and at other times badly, for most probably a mixture of both. The first stage he calls Trust vs. Mistrust.

Trust

Erikson proposes that the issue which has to be worked through is one of learning to trust in mother, in the small world encompassing the baby, and through such trust to have faith in one's own being. This stage lays the foundation for trust and faith in succeeding stages of life . . . If there is a failure in nurturing be it accidental or deliberate, the outcome for the baby is likely to be one of mistrust, an inability to believe either in others or in one's basic self. Such an outcome inevitably weakens the facility with which a person copes with the developmental tasks of the next stage, where physical developments necessitate dealing with new issues. [11]

If the womb was a comfortable, safe haven, the learning of basic trust will have begun there and will continue in a more obvious way during this first stage of life. However it does not stop there. Trust is not just an issue of the first stage but has to be continually renegotiated throughout life. But if the baby is securely and reliably cared for during the first six months he will grow naturally to trust his environment as good and feel himself to be good also. However, if there is failure in some way to meet the baby's needs the lesson learnt is not to trust but to mistrust.

Dr Lake suggests that the basic needs of the baby are unmet when the mother is unable or unwilling to give herself constantly to the baby during the waking hours of the first weeks and months. 'Babies,' he says, 'live as persons and grow in basic trust in so far as they can live in the reliable presence of the mother. It is that which builds up a sound self-hood and human being-as-a-person.' In fact he goes on to say that well-being and the sense of 'how good and glorious it is to be me' are derived from the times the baby spends looking up at a loving and adoring countenance. 'These are basic needs. It is part of the parental contract to meet these needs.' However, should the baby be left to scream for longer than is bearable, Dr Lake believes that 'the baby is pushed progressively, by loss of trust and hope, into despair. Finally, if the situation goes on too long and no one comes "in time", there is a fall into dread, disintegration, death of the self, and nothingness.'[12]

Freud's phrase 'His Majesty, the Baby' is appropriate for these early months. It is every baby's right, for a few months, to think that the world revolves around him and his needs. This omnipotence should only diminish gradually.

At about six months the task of separating from mother must start; it is continued through subsequent stages and only to be finally achieved when the child reaches maturity.

Separation

At first, in the baby's immature mind he is inseparable from mother. It is a stage of symbiosis (oneness). The mother goes along with this and only gradually, with father's help, draws back from this oneness, coinciding with the baby's growing ability to distinguish her as a separate person from himself.

It is sometimes difficult for the mother to withdraw from her total preoccupation with the baby. In this case the father must assist her to do so by helping her to begin the separation and gradually resume her place beside him once again. This separation does not mean the baby will cease to be dependent on or attached to the mother, but as mother begins to give up this 'primary maternal preoccupation' an element of disappointment and frustration will enter the baby's life. 'The good-enough mother' is a term coined by Winnicott and it is especially in the last phase of stage one that mother needs to be 'good-enough' rather than 'too good' or 'too bad'.

Internalisation

Another task for the baby is to internalise his mother. At first baby sees mother as part of himself, but at the same time an internalising process has begun which continues right on through childhood. A baby may go through a stage of crying whenever mother leaves the room. He has not yet reached the stage when he can hold a picture of mother inside himself. When she is lost to sight she is totally lost to him. Gradually, however, the baby begins to have a sense of her presence even when she is not there. When she leaves the room, this will mean that she is only momentarily lost to sight and not gone for ever.

It is this 'internalised mother' that helps the baby make the transition from oneness to separateness. A child who has not adequately achieved this is often very insecure and needs to keep mother in view all the time. He is miserable when she is not there and can be extremely clinging when she is there, long beyond the stage when separateness should be possible.

A major interruption of the love process in the first year will cause this type of insecurity. A lovely family I once met had adopted a beautiful Asian child. She had suffered the terrible trauma of separation and loss of all her family in the first year of life. At the time of our meeting she was about fourteen and seemed a happy, gifted teenager. I was interested to hear, however, that she had reacted badly when her mother had gone back to work for a short time. Though the mother had left for work after the children had left for school and returned before they did, the child did not cope well with not having Mummy in her usual place – at home.

She appeared to be stuck at the point of the past trauma.
Her parents had disappeared before she had been fully able
to internalise them and part of her emotional development
had been stunted at this point. Now at fourteen she had not
managed to internalise her adopted mother sufficiently to
feel secure when she could not visualise her at home. It was
as if her mother ceased to exist when she was lost to sight,
as had sadly been the case with her real parents.

When the task of internalising is achieved mother can be
absent for short periods at first and then longer ones without
causing too great an insecurity in the baby.

Results of failure in this stage

Certain unavoidable mistakes in an otherwise secure
childhood will not greatly affect a child's future. But
continual failure in meeting basic needs creates a foundation
of mistrust and fear, the results of which are seen in
counselling rooms daily.

Painful dependency needs

Such a traumatised baby may suffer from painful
dependency needs in later life or show signs of real
separation-anxiety. This can cause panic attacks when alone,
in large open spaces or unfamiliar places. When the need
to be held in babyhood is not sufficiently met the adult may
find that he or she is left with a longing to be held by a
woman. Frequently this is mistakenly interpreted as an erotic
or sexual need.

On one occasion a woman was being prayed for by
another woman during a public service. On being asked what
she was feeling, she replied with shame and embarrassment,
'I keep wanting you to hold me.' Another counselee
admitted to us that she was afraid of having lesbian

tendencies because she responded with such hunger every time a woman embraced her. Her own mother had not been affectionate and had never satisfied her daughter's need for nurture.

Mistrust of other people

Another painful effect of trauma during this stage is a commitment-anxiety, such as that found in the 'schizoid' personality. This is different from schizophrenia which Frank Lake describes as 'a molecular splitting or fragmentation of mind' in which delusions and hallucinations are common. The 'schizoid' personality develops as a consequence of overwhelming infantile trauma in which the ego splits. This may be due to an extremely painful delivery or to the 'too-prolonged absence of the mother who is the necessary personal source of being'.[13] The 'schizoid' personality has passed the margin of wanting and has lost the desire to relate, to be touched, held, attended to. In contrast to the 'hysterical' personality, whose whole desire is to have someone to be with him, touch him and hold him, the schizoid wants to be left to live a life of un-relatedness to others. It is a position of total mistrust. What he learned in the early months he continues to project on to anyone trying to come close.

A little boy I know had very traumatic beginnings to his life and spent his early years with a child-minder because his mother had to work. He has always found it difficult to look into anyone's eyes, especially his mother's. He told her one day that he hated her going away from him. He hated it when he was a baby and hates it now. He told her that when he looks at her it hurts him, especially if he looks into her eyes. 'Sometimes,' he said, 'I think you must be evil because my stomach feels as if it is going to explode when I look at you.' Here we can see the beginnings of the schizoid split. The pain of being left and needing his mother caused this child to turn away from her, the very person he wanted to relate to. Fortunately for this little boy his mother now has a good understanding of his problems and is well on the road to helping him come to terms with his feelings.

Self-doubt

Through the reliable, loving presence of mother a baby learns to trust his environment, other people and also himself. The absence of a reliable mother causes the foundations of the personality to be insecure. This can result in indecisiveness, a low sense of self-worth and self-doubt.

Biographer Alison Miller writes about Ludovic Kennedy's grief at the cold relationship he had with his mother. Miller quotes him as saying, 'My most abiding fear . . . was of my mother. To say she did not love me is questionable. But to say that she never gave any outward sign of loving me is to state no more than a fact. At the age of 69 it may sound ridiculous to record that after babyhood (and for all I know during it) my mother never once showed me by a kiss or a cuddle the slightest vestige of physical affection, but that is how it was. When, later in life, I read of Freud's theory that a boy who has been truly loved by his mother never has self-doubts, I found an explanation for all my youthful agonies of indecision.'[14]

Depression

A sudden loss of intimacy with a good mother figure during this first stage may result in an underlying feeling of depression and hopelessness in an otherwise healthy adult.

A drastic loss of accustomed mother-love without proper substitution at this time can lead (under otherwise aggravating conditions) to acute infantile depression or to a mild but chronic stage of mourning which may give a depressive under-tone to the whole remainder of life. But even under the most favourable circumstances, this stage leaves a residue of a primary sense of evil and doom and of a universal nostalgia for a lost paradise. [15]

A 'lost paradise' describes the experience of a baby who loses too soon the intimacy and closeness of the maternal presence. The source of goodness has disappeared and a sense of loss ensues which may linger on, colouring the rest of life.

Dr John White refers to the many studies done which link childhood bereavement with depression in adult life. Though it was found that childhood bereavement does not necessarily produce adult depression, it is a powerful influence. Dr White comments on the relationship between the age at which the bereavement occurred and the number of patients who became depressed. 'Most of the depressed patients experienced bereavement during the first four years of life, a smaller number between the ages of five and nine, and the smallest number between ten and fourteen.' [16]

It would seem therefore that any loss of mother-love at this early stage carries with it the possibility of depression in later life.

By the end of the baby's first year a great deal has been accomplished and the baby should be ready for the next phase in his development. However, failure to negotiate this first stage successfully may leave a person with some difficulties that still limit his life in the present. But with patient persistence all need not be lost.

'Perseverance must finish its work so that you may be mature and complete, not lacking anything' (Jam.1:4). When Jacob met his brother Esau after a long estrangement he wrestled all night with God. Just before day-break the man (God) said, 'Let me go, for it is daybreak.' But Jacob replied, 'I will not let you go unless you bless me'

(Gen.32:26). Jacob was determined to hang on to God until finally God blessed him. To be healed of the effects of failure in this early stage may take time, patience and determination. You may need to repeat the exercises several times and to stay with number four for several weeks, coming back to it whenever you feel insecure.

Exercises

1. Ask yourself the following questions:
Do I find it easy to trust others, myself, God?
Is my body at peace with itself or do I suffer mysterious aches and pains?
Am I able to form intimate relationships with others?
Am I able to let those I love have the freedom to come and go as they need to?
Do I see myself as a person of worth?
Am I decisive?
Do I enjoy being touched affectionately by friends and family?
Does touch relax me?
Can I eat without binging?
Am I happy with my own company?

To score seven or more affirmatives means you were probably nurtured successfully by a 'good-enough mother'. To have five or more negatives will probably mean there were more failures than you could easily cope with.

2. With your friend/counsellor pray through each question that was answered negatively.

Take plenty of time and express to Jesus the feelings about each question. Tell Him how it feels to be touched, to trust others or to relate closely to another person.

Give yourself permission to express the feelings that arise. Remember the absence or loss of a trustworthy mother-figure must be grieved before it can be healed. 'Blessed are those who mourn, for they will be comforted' (Matt.5:4).

3. It would seem that most babies are born with their hearts wide open, rather like a camera. When the shutter opens an imprint of the presenting scene is impressed on the film inside. During the first year the baby is receiving pictures that are deeply imprinted on the subconscious. It is important to remember that whilst a child is a brilliant recorder he is often a bad interpreter. Many of the memories, therefore, may be incorrectly interpreted. Only God can show you the truth and replace the lie.

As you grieve the loss of nurture as a small child and feel the pain of the bad pictures that were recorded, the shutter of your heart will open and you can ask God to replace the old imprints with new ones.

'God is love' (1 Jn.4:8).

'God is light' (1 Jn.1:5).

King David prayed, 'Let the light of your face shine upon us, O Lord' (Ps.4:6).

And 'The Lord said to Moses, "Tell Aaron and his sons, 'This is how you are to bless the Israelites,' Say to them: 'The Lord bless you and keep you; the Lord make his face shine upon you and be gracious to you; the Lord turn his face towards you and give you peace'." ' (Num.6:22–6).

Look up into His face and receive the imprint of His light and love.

4. God knows how to nurture a baby. Spend time with God allowing Him to mother you.

'Can a mother forget the baby at her breast and have no compassion on the child she has borne? Though she may forget, I will not forget you! See, I have engraved you on the palms of my hands' (Isa.49:15,16).

'The Lord your God is with you, he is mighty to save. He will take great delight in you, he will quiet you with his love, he will rejoice over you with singing' (Zeph.3:17).

God's complete understanding of Motherhood is shown in His words to those who love Jerusalem.

'For you will nurse and be satisfied at her comforting breasts; you will drink deeply and delight in her overflowing abundance. For this is what the Lord says: "I will extend peace to her like a river, and the wealth of nations like a flooding stream; you will nurse and be carried on her arm and dandled on her knees. As a mother comforts her child, so will I comfort you; and you will be comforted over Jerusalem" ' (Isa.66:11–13).

5. Remember that releasing forgiveness to those who have failed you is part of the healing process.

6. THE AGE OF DISCOVERY
(Second stage, 15 months−3 years)

'The childhood shows the man; as morning shows the day.' (Milton's *Paradise Regained*)

There is an old familiar story of two shoe salesmen visiting similar third-world countries and wiring back to their separate headquarters. One sent the message: 'Natives have no shoes at all. Send shipload at once'. The other said, 'Natives do not wear shoes. Returning home immediately.' Like these two men we all tend to see life through differently coloured spectacles. It may be the same situation we are viewing but our lenses are coloured by our personal and individual experience of life. The foundations laid in this second phase of childhood will help determine our attitudes to life around us. In the first stage the foundations for forming close relationships were being laid. Now the child begins to look beyond Mummy's face to life beyond her. By still keeping her in view he has the confidence and courage to begin an exciting journey of discovery.

By one year most babies are crawling and some even walking. Certainly by fifteen months a normal baby is off in all directions. Most mothers look back at this time in sheer amazement that both she and the toddler survived. Our third daughter, Becky, was particularly inquisitive and therefore more accident-prone than the others. As a child in Chile she survived plugging a metal fork into an electric socket, a dangerous fall out of a high-chair, a rush to hospital to have her stomach pumped out after the consumption of suspected poison – not to mention nearly dying with peritonitis. I used to lie awake at night wondering if either of us would live to see her teens!

Because it would be easy to get lost in the maze of nappies, potties, toys, accidents and sticky fingers, I will try and find a way through this frantic stage by asking three key questions: what are the major developmental tasks of the child at this stage? What part do parents play? And lastly, what could go wrong?

Providing the baby has reached a stage of sufficient trust in his environment and in particular with his 'good-enough mother' he will have the secure base he needs for moving gradually into this next stage. If, however, some foundations of mistrust have been laid and there has been a failure in 'the holding environment' (Winnicott's term for the security surrounding a baby), the baby will experience difficulty moving on and may find the different tasks frightening and frustrating when they could be exciting and stimulating for him.

The task of the baby

Independence

According to Erikson the issue that has to be resolved here is one of autonomy versus shame and doubt. The definition for autonomy is 'The right of self-government; personal freedom; freedom of the will.'[1] It is obviously ridiculous to suggest that any two-year-old child has reached the stage of self-government. He will be under his parents' authority and care for many more years to come. The point, however, is not that the infant becomes self-governing in the near future but that the child should begin to develop initiative and independence. Already he is able to differentiate between himself and his mother and he is forming a picture of himself apart from her. He can find his nose, his eyes, his ears and his toes. Alternately he can point to his mother's nose, ears, eyes and toes. His own self-image is forming and by the end of this second stage he should have developed a separate personal identity which is expressed in the little word 'I'. His conversation will be dotted with, 'I am's', 'I can's', and 'I have's'.

He is beginning to make choices on his own and has likes and dislikes which he communicates in no uncertain terms. The word 'no' is frequently on his lips. 'Temper, stubbornness, resistance and rebellion are normal and desirable and their absence is a cause for concern, often indicating that energy and drive needed later for initiative and independent functioning have become blocked.'[2]

Control

Freud called this the 'anal' phase. The expression could give the impression that this stage is taken up solely with toilet-training. In part this is true and certainly in the past this was seen as the main issue. Mother felt she had failed if little Suzie was not out of nappies by two years old. However, the issue really is not only one of bladder and bowel control but of control generally. By his first birthday baby discovers he can hold things and then let them go. Mummy begins the tiresome task of pushing the pram and picking up poor teddy every few yards. The bottle or drinking cup can be held or dropped at will. This is the time of the sticky kitchen floor!

The toddler is gaining more and more control over his movements. He crawls, he stands and then suddenly he walks. At the end of the second year the child is ready for a tentative and gradual introduction to the potty. Part of learning control is the realisation that he can do it or hold it back at will. A child who is struggling for autonomy and independence may well make this the place to battle it out

with mother. On the other hand the nervous, timid child
may desperately want to please but anxiety may lead to
accidents and loss of control.

A strict regime of toilet training usually leads to problems.
The less Mummy worries the easier it will be. I did
unnecessary battle with my first child and the process was
surrounded with tension and frustration. When the others
came along I decided to be more South American in my
approach and I relaxed! The whole procedure was quite
simple. I realised that when a child is able and ready to learn
he will take these steps in his stride, naturally and easily,
so long as he is not pressurised. 'Pressure for self-control
and conformity before the genetic pattern has unfolded to
a point where this is appropriate, or encouragement of
self-indulgence at an age where self-control should be
developing, can be as harmful as failure of the parents to
respond at all.'[3]

Discovery

As I write this I can hear one-year-old Philip galloping on
all fours across the landing towards my study door. He is
on a journey of discovery. Life is exciting, interesting and
full of surprises. (For both Philip and his grandmother!)

If a solid foundation of trust and security has been laid
in the first year, discovery will automatically follow. If the
baby has not experienced a good strong 'holding
environment' in the first year he will tend to mistrust every
new experience and confront everything strange and
different with fear.

The clinging, whining child is simply manifesting mistrust
of his surroundings. Where he has not negotiated the first
phase sufficiently he will be unprepared for the momentous
step of letting Mummy go and discovering the fascinating
things around him. Michael Jacobs refers to 'the many
"little deaths" that accompany different stages of life, from

the letting go of the security of the womb to the letting go that leads to the tomb. Nearly every change involves a loss as well as a potential gain.'[4]

Any major disruption in the child's familiar pattern of life and in particular of his relationship with mother will cause him to forgo his exploratory behaviour and regress to a stage of clinging attachment. An infant cannot concentrate on the task of discovery if he is preoccupied with his mother's whereabouts or his fear of her disappearance. Even the most secure child will enjoy this phase far more if Mummy remains available and near at hand. 'When mother is present or her whereabouts well-known and is willing to take part in friendly interchange, a child usually ceases to show attachment behaviour and, instead, explores his environment. In such a situation mother can be regarded as providing her child with a secure base from which to explore and to which he can return, especially should he become tired or frightened.'[5]

Language

A year-old child needs plenty of communication. His understanding of words is growing daily, though he may not be able to say much more than 'Da, da' for everything. He is becoming adept at making his needs known and does not have to rely totally on his parents' intuitive understanding of his needs. Repetition delights him and he needs to hear the same songs and phrases over and over.

Over the last few months breakfast time in our home has been accompanied by Grandpa singing 'Two little eyes to look to God' and Philip chuckling with pleasure and blocking his ears when it comes to 'two little ears to hear God's word'. Later there is the daily routine of counting the dogs on the kitchen poster and touching each one.

The learning of language aids self-control and self-determination. A parent repeatedly points to dangerous objects saying, 'No, baby not to touch' and if it is something hot and likely to burn this is accompanied with 'ss, ss – hot'. As language develops the toddler uses the words he has heard to help control himself. He will toddle up to the oven and his little head will start shaking and he can be overheard saying to himself, 'No, no, ss, ss.' Also a degree of self-determinations comes with language. 'Dink' shouted loudly will usually produce the required drink of juice.

Words are an important part of communication, though not the only means. Good foundations are being laid at this age though both too much pressure to perform or too little stimulation can hinder the development of normal communication.

The parents' task

What does a child require from his parents in order for him to negotiate this stage of development successfully?

Good boundaries

No child of this age can set his own boundaries or sense his own limitations. This has to be done for him. As the maintainer and protector of the family boundaries father now begins to take a more prominent part in the infant's life. Until this time the child has not needed much discipline and so Dad's main concern has been with supporting Mummy and helping her in the care of baby (or the other children) when necessary. From now on discipline and control will become constant issues and if mother has to decide them and implement them on her own she will soon feel worn out.

The reason for defining limits and setting boundaries is to give the child the best possible environment for his task of discovery and exploration. 'From the parent, the child at this stage needs clear and definite limits, both adequately wide (to allow him to experiment and learn how to control these new powers) and sufficiently firm (to provide a safe container within which the new energies can be released without too much fear).'[6]

Establishing boundaries is a major concern at this stage, and normal safety measures will ensure, as much as possible, that the infant is physically secure.

Emotional security

As we have seen, mother's reliable presence gives the baby confidence for exploration. Following research on students who appeared to their teachers to be of good general mental health and who promised well as leaders and community workers, it was found that, 'In almost every case both parents were still alive. The typical picture presented was of a happy peaceful home in which both parents shared responsibilities and interests, and were regarded by the children as loving and giving. During childhood, they said, they had felt with mother, above everything else, secure. At the same time they had identified strongly with father.'[7]

This stage is marked more by activity than passivity and it is hard to keep some children still long enough to give them cuddles. Nevertheless children, whatever their size, still need plenty of physical contact with both mother and father. It may come in the form of a romp with Daddy before bath-time, or a story and cuddle with Mummy before being tucked up in bed. However it comes ongoing physical affection is vital for the child's well-being.

Stimulation

Fathers may feel unnecessary extras with regard to the upbringing of children. But Winnicott demonstrates convincingly that a father's input is very necessary to the child; not as a duplication of mother but in its own right. Part of the importance lies in the fact that 'though father is a familiar figure, he is essentially different from the mother out of whom the infant has grown'. In order to give a sense of security the mother in one sense has to be slightly boring in her relationship with the baby. As we have said 'only on a basis of monotony can a mother profitably add richness'.[8] The father brings excitement and variety into the child's life; his games are different, more boisterous and exciting; his stories are often more interesting and full of new ideas, stimulating and enlarging the infant's horizons.

As this stage unfolds the child will gradually become aware of the difference between mother and father. If he is allowed to enjoy and experience this difference he will naturally commence the transition into the next stage of development when he will begin to establish his own sexual identity. As Robin Skynner explains to John Cleese, 'The child needs parents who share some activities and interests, and at least some of his care. But the child also needs them to be different, and stand for different things and to respect and enjoy and admire each other's differences. You need two landmarks to get a bearing and find out where you are — and you need them to be a certain distance apart.'[9]

Toys geared to the child's age will also provide stimulation, as will repetitive songs and games. The occasional company of other children is important too, providing mother is around to provide safety. Though relating and playing with other children will not fully come until the next stage, the child still needs the stimulation and awareness of others. Even at eighteen months a child will begin to express affection towards a baby and respond to other children with interest. Our last baby was born when number three was eighteen months and I remember being amazed at the affection Becky expressed for the baby and the tender way she touched her.

Space

The preoccupation with boundaries, control and safety should not interfere with the child's needs for space in which to explore. Some parents are so nervous they curtail the child's activities to such an extent that his development is impeded. I have never yet met a normal, lively toddler who was happy to sit in a playpen for hours on end. We tried to use one and found it only caused misery and frustration. It is relatively simple to ensure one 'child-proof' room and a child of two is fairly easy to distract when intent on playing with some forbidden object. Substitution is always better than blocking at this age and avoids unnecessary clashes of will.

If the objective is development of the child's autonomy and the discovery of himself and his environment, then he needs both physical space and emotional space. In order for the child to differentiate between himself and his mother it is important that she continues to withdraw from her total involvement with him, giving him space to develop as an individual person. Robin Skynner frequently underlines the important part the father plays in helping the mother to return by stages to her primary investment in the marital relationship, rather than in the child. 'It is perhaps this crucial function of the father in assisting the mother and child to grow apart progressively, thereby facilitating self-definition and independence, which makes the presence and active involvement of the father so important.'[10]

Disappointment

By this stage 'His Majesty, the baby' should have toppled from his throne and be well on the way to becoming an ordinary subject — the child of simply a 'good-enough mother'. This is in fact achieved as mother fails a little and consequently disappoints the child now and again.

Our grandson, Philip, dominates the attention of every adult in sight. He constantly looks to see if we are admiring and watching his latest trick. He woos us with his smiles and chuckles. He could be in danger of staying too long in the stage of Mr Omnipotent except that his mother has a new baby to occupy her time besides friends who call and distract her attention from him for short moments. So Philip suffers occasional disappointment and frustration and through these experiences he will gradually become accustomed to sharing the limelight with others.

Failure in this stage and its possible results

Daily in our counselling room we meet those who have failed for different reasons and to varying degrees to negotiate this exciting stage of development. What sort of things can commonly go wrong?

Incomplete separation from mother

This problem may arise if the mother needs the baby to give her a sense of identity and to fulfil her own need for intimacy which for some reason she has not achieved with her husband. Or another reason may be that the mother, being emotionally damaged herself, has projected her own fear of separation on to her baby.

In later life this can produce problems and it is common to meet people in their twenties, thirties, forties and even fifties, who are still controlled by their mother's need of them. One young man at a conference recently told me of his struggle with homosexual feelings. Apparently, though now in his twenties, he was still trying to leave home but felt guilty because he was sure his mother would not be able to cope without him. Equal difficulties accompany girls who have not separated from their mothers. One recently told me of the difficulty she had with making decisions — even when buying simple things for her own wardrobe. Her mother had always shopped with her and been there to help her. Though her mother had recently died and she was now physically separated, she remained dependent upon her emotionally.

Too much or too little attention

An adult who suffers from more than ordinary needs for support or undivided attention from others is still emotionally stuck at the stage of wanting mother and father's undivided attention. Attention-seeking in an adult usually goes back to either too much or too little attention in childhood. Mr Omnipotent may have been allowed to outlive his welcome. Either his parents had too carefully avoided ever disappointing him so that he had now become unreasonable in his demands for attention or he was disappointed too early and too often and was left hungering desperately for more!

Inconsistent caregiving

Though the infant needs to gain independence from mother and to separate from her, he needs her to be reliably present in order for him to do it. Her presence gives the child the courage to explore and try out new exploits. Her absence turns his world into a strange, frightening place. An asthmatic child I knew had his first attack as a two-year-old when his mother suddenly disappeared into hospital.

We all handle new situations better when people we know are around us, but for a person deprived of consistent care during childhood a major problem of insecurity can be the result. Such people are often plagued with a fear of the unknown or the unfamiliar. Even going on holiday can be a problem. Such a person may be either clinging and dependent in relationships or conversely independent and anti-social. In both cases fear of loss or separation governs this behaviour.

Though an absent caregiver may have very good reasons for being absent the child is left with feelings of anxiety, anger, rejection, even hate. The story of Reggie illustrates the ambivalent feelings experienced by a child when a relationship he depends upon is broken. Reggie had spent most of his life in a nursery and while there he formed two close relationships with two young nurses who took care of him at different times. His attachment to one of these, his 'own' nurses, was suddenly broken at two years and eight months when she married. He was completely bewildered and desperate after she had gone. A fortnight later, when she visited him, he refused to look at her. He turned his head to the other side when she spoke to him, but stared at the closed door after she had left the room. In bed that evening he sat up and said: 'My very own Mary-Ann! But I don't like her' (Burlingham and Freud 1944).[11]

An eleven-year-old boy wrote an expressive poem while in therapy. His mother had died when he was fifteen months old after which he experienced several substitute mothers.

Jumbo had a baby dressed in green,
Wrapped it up in paper and sent it to the Queen.
The Queen did not like it because it was too fat,
She cut it up in pieces and gave it to the cat.
The cat did not like it because it was too thin,
She cut it up in pieces and gave it to the King.
The King did not like it because he was too slow,
Threw it out the window and gave it to the crow.[12]

On another occasion when his therapist was going on holiday he expressed his despair of ever being loved in the words of a traditional ditty:

Oh, my little darling, I love you;
Oh, my little darling, I don't believe you do.
If you really loved me, as you say you do,
You would not go to America and leave me at the Zoo.[13]

Feelings of anger, rejection and hate may lie dormant within a person who has been deprived of consistent caregiving. These often surface later in life when there is the possibility or danger of forming an attachment to someone. Ambivalent feelings of love and hate may then plague the relationship.

Lack of parental support

When learning new skills an infant needs constant praise and encouragement. Lack of interest or criticism push the child into a hopeless sense of failure. His mind becomes absorbed with negative thoughts about himself and the world around him.

Another threat to a child's worth is being laughed at or shamed by the adults around him. Growing up can become acutely difficult for the child who is laughed at and derided by the adults he lives with. This will adversely effect his long-term view of himself.

Kenneth Rose writes of Lord Curzon's childhood and the bitter shame he experienced at the hands of his governess. The memory of this remained with Curzon long after the events, and who knows how much they contributed to his difficult personality later in life. His own description of this time is harrowing.

She persecuted and beat us in the most cruel way . . . tied us for long hours to chairs . . . shut us up in darkness . . . wounded our pride by dressing us (me in particular) in red shining calico petticoats . . . with an immense conical cap on our heads round which, as well as on our breast and backs, were sewn strips of paper bearing in enormous characters, written by ourselves, the words Liar, Sneak, Coward, Lubber and the like. In this guise she compelled us to go out . . . at even distances and show ourselves to the gardeners . . . and to show ourselves to the villagers.[14]

Self-confidence is not something people are born with; it develops in a loving, encouraging environment. It is destroyed in a harsh and critical one.

Excessive control

'Spare the rod and spoil the child' was the dictum many parents used to bring up their children. Though every child needs to learn obedience, the way this is taught can be either helpful or harmful.

Excessive control and harsh discipline is not a good soil for the tender spirit of a child to grow up in and this is seen by the fruit that develops later.

Such parental behaviour often produces an over-controlled adult who lives his life by rules and regulations. He may have left home and be far away from the critical parent, but having internalised his controlling parent he cannot leave him/her behind, and continues living as if the parent was still present to be pleased. He may even project his need to placate his parent on to God and become a very legalistic Christian, fearful of displeasing the harsh, cruel God he has perceived.

Another result can be the adult who rebels against control and almost deliberately lacks discipline in his life. A friend of mine used always to be late for every appointment. The rest of her life appeared to be organised and tidy. It was hard to understand this attitude until I realised that her father had been in the army and had been very particular about punctuality; so much so that the clocks in his home were always five minutes fast. Though my friend loved and respected her father her lateness was an unspoken gesture of rebellion against his excessive control of her time.

Inconsistent control and weak boundaries

When caregivers fail to make a child's environment safe by putting in controls and safe boundaries the resulting fear and insecurity may create an adult who later needs to over-control his environment. This may be by perfectionism or some kind of obsessive behaviour.

Weak boundaries leave a child uncertain of how far he can go. He may later live as if there were no boundaries at all. One man I know grew up with a father who had abdicated his position of authority to the mother. Unfortunately she was too busy and too tired to give her lively son consistent discipline, so he was allowed to run wild. By the time he was a young adult he was in trouble with the law and seemed unable to control his life. As the years went by his troubles multiplied. Now in his late fifties he is in debt, has problems with alcohol abuse and his third wife is threatening to leave him.

It is so important, especially for boys, that the father sets good, reasonable and firm boundaries. In years to come this will have more benefit than any of the expensive presents many children enjoy today.

Jealousy and sibling rivalry

The most likely time for the arrival of another baby is during this second phase, between eighteen months and three years. However well parents try to prepare the toddler for the new arrival the toddler frequently reacts by being difficult. Some children regress and become very demanding and clinging. Others are aggressive, especially towards the new baby, and in some extreme cases a child will withdraw into himself and refuse to relate to anyone. Others are like one of our girls who decided the new baby belonged to her and became over-protective and responsible.

Though every child will handle the arrival of a brother or sister differently it is important to understand the enormous adaptation the child is having to make and that it will take time for him to come to terms with the 'little intruder'. Accepting the child's bad feelings and helping him to express them appropriately will help. A child can learn very early to suppress the 'unacceptable' feelings and show very little outward disturbance. Our oldest grandson was fairly good when his baby brother came along. He was occasionally a little rough with him and was maybe naughtier than usual, but on the surface appeared to be coping well. However, the bad feelings he was holding on to eventually came out. He awoke one night screaming and insisted that he had pulled his baby brother's head off. Believing he had thrown it into the corner of the kitchen he led his mother downstairs to show her the exact spot and it took a long time for him to accept that it had not really happened.

Possessiveness, jealousy and rivalry in adult relationships may be a hang-over related to that early stage of difficult transition from being Mummy's sole possession to sharing her attention with a baby. A feeling of always being overlooked, put on one side or taken advantage of by others may later accompany the adult who learned early to suppress such sibling jealousy.

A woman had had a problem with rejection all her school-days. As she talked and prayed with her counsellor the memory of her mother in hospital for the birth of her sister came to mind. She immediately began to cry expressing her pain at being overlooked by all the adoring adults crowding around her new baby sister.

Another, much older woman came to us suffering from depression and occasional outbursts of anger. The depression and the anger nearly always followed a time when she felt her family had failed to consider her or had completely ignored her feelings. The major upset in her childhood had also (as in the above example) been the arrival of her younger sister. As we prayed she had a picture of herself at the time of her sister's birth; seeing herself as left out in the cold, feeling one moment angry and the next sad and lonely.

Foundations are laid first in any building. They dictate the shape and strength of the eventual edifice. Faulty foundations will cause problems in the finished building. As we have seen the foundations laid in a child's early years can influence his behaviour in later life. Many of the problems we encounter are derived from early experiences.

The third and next stage is equally foundational but for different reasons.

Exercises

1. A failure to negotiate this stage of childhood properly may have left you with some unresolved difficulties. Can you identify with any of the following?
Homosexual fantasies
Indecisiveness
Fear of dependency
Abnormal feelings of guilt and responsibility
Insecurity in unusual or unfamiliar surroundings
Clinging to motherly figures
Difficulty separating from your mother
Ambivalent feelings towards those close to you
Negativity and self-criticisms
Lack of confidence
Over-controlling and obsessional behaviour
Lack of self-discipline
Jealousy of others
Attention-seeking

2. Pray with your friend/counsellor. Talk to God about the

things you identify with on the list, and ask Him to show you the root cause.

Describe aloud any specific memory that comes to your mind. Allow the feelings and thoughts surrounding the experience to surface and be expressed.

3. Then ask God to minister His healing to the memory. Give God plenty of time to do this.

4. Use your two-way diary to write down any irrational beliefs you have held. Give God time to reveal His truth to you and then write down what God has just said to you.

5. Remember that if our attitudes have been wrong repentance must be part of the healing process. 'Godly sorrow brings repentance that leads to salvation and leaves no regret' (2 Cor.7:10). Forgiveness of those who caused us hurt is also essential (Matt.6:14,15).

6. Continue to open up to God the painful memories from this period of your childhood. Don't be afraid to go through the process of grieving, but beware of self-pity.

7. Wrong behaviour patterns may have resulted in your life. If this is so seek ways to change them, and 'to put off your old self, which is being corrupted by its deceitful desires; to be made new in the attitude of your minds; and to put on the new self, created to be like God in true righteousness and holiness' (Eph.4:22,23).

8. If you are experiencing difficulty leaving home or detaching from your mother ask yourself the following questions:
Am I still emotionally dependent upon her?
Do I need her support?
Do I need her approval?
Is my life unmanageable without her?
Is the relationship with my mother a controlling influence in my life?

Do I need to separate from her?

9. If your answers are mostly in the affirmative perhaps the following exercise will be of help to you.

a) Close your eyes and visualise your mother and yourself together.

b) Ask God to show you in which ways you are still bound to her.

c) Ask God to give you the power to start breaking free.

d) In your imagination see yourself attached by a cord to your mother. The cord is made up of various strands. Take time to examine the strands and find out what they are.

e) Make a decision to be free. Now take a pair of scissors and cut the cord.

f) Visualise yourself as standing separate and free.

g) Ask Jesus to come and stand between your mother and yourself. 'If the Son sets you free, you will be free indeed' (Jn.8:36).

h) Take notice of the thoughts and the feelings you have as you become separated.

i) Write down these thoughts and feelings in your two-way diary. Give God time to respond to you. Write down what He says to you.

j) In your journal make a list of the differences between you and your mother.

k) In the coming week find one thing you can do that will break the old patterns and make the separation a fact in your life.

l) In doing this try not to be hurtful towards your mother but remember that you are not responsible for her bad feelings. Protecting someone from their bad feelings helps them to stay in a place of immaturity.

m) Spend time thanking God for your mother and for the individual, separate lives He has given you.

7. SEXUALITY EXPLOITED OR EXPLORED
(Third stage, 3–6 years)

'The basis of the family is the relationship between parents themselves.' Madeleine Davis and David Wallbridge[1]

Some married friends of ours once asked a child specialist what they could do to make their children feel secure. 'Love one another,' was his reply. We will appreciate the wisdom of this remark more fully as we look at the needs of a child, including the child we once were, in this third stage of development. As we have seen, trust and dependence are the dominant features of the early months of everyone's life. Though a father has an important role from the beginning his presence comes into greater focus during the second stage when boundaries and control are becoming important issues. In the third stage the maturing child is ready for the complexities of relating to a couple, namely his parents, with whom he has already formed good individual ties.

St Luke's account of the birth and childhood of Jesus is significant. Immediately after the birth of Jesus Mary is mentioned as caring for the baby: 'and she gave birth to her firstborn, a son. She wrapped him in cloths and placed him in a manger, because there was no room for them in the inn' (2:7). As the narrative progresses Joseph and Mary are coupled together more frequently. But once Jesus is older Luke refers to 'his parents'. Three times St Luke mentions Mary and Joseph together, calling them 'his parents', at the same time Jesus is depicted as becoming separate from them and we see him relating outside the family.

'We are born not knowing that we are separate from our mothers. Slowly we discover this, and begin the hard task of separating our personal and sexual identities from hers.'[2] By the end of the second phase this hard task should be accomplished and the child should have established a personal identity of his own. Between three and four years the sexual identity will be decided and a boy, for example, will know that he belongs on Daddy's side of the line; the opposite to his mother. A little girl will know she is on her mother's side; the opposite to her father.

My three-year-old grandson made a profound statement about his six-month-old brother. 'Sam is a boy now,' he said to me. 'What was he before?' I asked, surprised. Ashley thought for a while and then said quite seriously, 'A baby.' For a while I couldn't understand why Sam's sexuality had suddenly become determined for Ashley. It then dawned on me that Ashley was in fact reflecting his own growing sexual awareness. He was beginning to line people up on different sides of the fence. 'That person is a boy like me and that one is a girl like Mummy.' He was on target in his sexual development.

Sexual dysfunction may result if, for any reason, this development is blocked or inadequately completed. Though the sexual identity should be more or less decided by the beginning of the third stage it will be built on and the roles developed over the next few years. With this in view there are several important issues to be examined.

Issues for the child

The relationship to parents

In the early months and years a baby enjoys a very simple form of relating on an almost exclusively one to one basis.

He has enjoyed being the centre of attention. As he matures the baby's ability to cope with separating from mother and including others in the relationship grows. He is learning to give up his omnipotence. This increasing maturity will enable him to cope with more complex relationships. He is able to suffer some exclusion and consequent jealousy in his relationship with his parents. His growing sense of personal identity enables him to view them as a couple who are united together and from whose presence he is sometimes excluded. This reinforces and helps him to continue the task of separating from mother and gives him his first important lessons in sharing and taking turns. It is all good preparation for starting school and making friends.

For a time it is right and proper for a baby to have the world revolve around him. It will build in good foundations for security and self-worth. However, this state of affairs should not continue for longer than is healthy and right. The parents must extricate themselves from the position of being obedient slaves, jumping to his every command and denying their own needs in favour of his. If they do not disaster will result.

I once visited a house where the father behaved like a tyrant. He demanded his meals when he felt like them and did not take into account the rest of the family. He was given his own preferred menu; the TV programmes were of his choosing and frequently the set was turned off with no consideration for others watching. I suspect he had had a slave instead of a mother!

Adults who exhibit unhealthy characteristics in relationships such as the need always to be the centre of attention, or relate in a possessive and jealous manner have most likely become stuck at the stage of relating exclusively to one individual at a time and never conquered the task of learning to relate to a couple.

An interest in the genitals

Freud called this period the 'genital stage' partly because around this age a child discovers those interesting parts of his anatomy and begins to enjoy the nice feelings they give him. He becomes aware of the physical distinctions between the sexes and will explore the difference given a chance! This is very innocent and based purely on quite normal curiosity rather than any sexual drive. When handled sensibly and naturally, only commenting when the child has stepped over the line of social propriety, this exploration of himself and others will add to the child's growing sexual identity and the taking up of male or female roles.

Just the other day five of our grandsons were playing in the paddling pool in the nude. While the children remained in the garden no one showed any concern over their state of undress. However, when they came into the house for tea my daughter suggested the boys put their pants back on. 'Why?' asked the five-year-old. 'Because you are too big now to run around the house without clothes,' she explained. Decency then prevailed without any condemnation or shaming of the child's sexuality.

Flirting with the opposite-sex parent

This third stage is also marked by an 'Oedipal conflict'. Oedipus, according to Greek mythology, unknowingly killed his father and married his mother. A child's growing sexuality will cause him or her to flirt with the parent of the opposite sex. We find little Danny having crossed over the line, firmly standing on Daddy's side and facing Mummy, who has until now been the only woman in his life. He becomes Daddy's rival for her affection and tries by hook or by crook to get her attention and separate her from his father. He cuddles and kisses her, wants her to spend time putting him to bed, telling him stories and remaining by his bedside while he goes to sleep. In the night, for whatever reason, he will often come into their bed and physically separate them by lying between them.

This is all normal behaviour and will be part of healthy development providing mother responds correctly. He needs to get the message that Mummy loves him, welcomes his attentions, and admires his masculinity but that she belongs to Daddy and is not available for an intimate, exclusive relationship. In this way he receives affirmation of his sexuality and does not have to be afraid of it or feel guilty about it as he would if mother responded inappropriately. In other words the most damaging thing is for him to win and become mother's 'little darling' or 'little husband'. Sexual and identity confusion will be the result of such an incestuous relationship.

The same applies to a little girl who flirts with Daddy, sitting on his lap, doing his hair, kissing and cuddling him. She needs to try out her female powers of attraction on him and to receive the message back that she is gorgeous and he finds her very attractive, but that any intimate sexual relationship is totally out of the question: only Mummy has a right to that. In this way the girl's sexuality is affirmed but by losing the contest against Mummy she doesn't have to carry guilt around or fear of retaliation, which would inhibit and damage her developing sexuality.

In our study of child development we need to draw attention to the place of the Oedipus complex in the emotional development of the three to five-year-old. 'Parental understanding can be a great aid in helping the child to successful resolution of the conflicts of this age.'[3]

The parental task

Though this stage is a difficult and hazardous one for the child if badly handled and failure could result in problems later in life, the task for the parents is straightforward. The important thing is to keep to the simple rules and not give way to a child who will try anything once and twice if he wins. To help the child negotiate this stage certain basic facts must be established by the parents.

God comes first

Parents who demonstrate faith in a loving God and live upright and moral lives are passing on a precious heritage to their children. First the child has the security of knowing that God's love surrounds him and his family. Secondly he is secure in the knowledge that his parents have chosen to place themselves and their family behind safe moral boundaries. A child needs to know that these boundaries are in place for very good reasons and that they are non-negotiable. Sexual immorality, witchcraft, blasphemy, filthy talk, lies, cheating and stealing are issues over which every Christian parent should stand firm. In the first place he needs to demonstrate the benefit and strength of these boundaries in his own life, and then, having encouraged the child through example, should consistently teach them throughout childhood. Explanation and discussion have their place, but rejection of parental standards and faith during the teens is often the result of too much 'preaching it' and not enough 'living it' by parents in these early years. Children are quick to spot inconsistency and insincerity. Later when peer pressure is strong the respect and love a child has for his parents will often be decisive factors in keeping him from yielding to such pressure.

Mother and father are in control

Besides living within God's boundaries and continuing the maintenance of boundaries for safety reasons, the boundaries around the parents' relationship need to be firmly in place and maintained. A child can quickly disrupt this relationship and set parents against each other. For his security and peace of mind he needs to know his parents are a united force and he is not powerful enough to divide them. It is too frightening for a child to even suspect he may have the power to separate his parents.

Sex is good

In this third period, 'the child not only has to accept that the parents are more powerful, but that they have a special relationship with each other and enjoy some pleasurable and indeed profoundly exciting activity from which he or she is excluded'.[4]

During these formative years a child is receiving a model for marriage. His impressions will most likely stay with him for the rest of his life. For the child to get good healthy messages about his own sexuality and sex in general there needs to be a relaxed, natural show of affection between his parents. Embarrassment or disgust are quickly spotted and a wrong message about sex received without a word being spoken. Pleasure and delight are equally easy to spot and are recorded in a child's memory and brought out at a later date when needed.

A woman came to see me once about her inability to find pleasure in making love to her husband. Before she was married she had slept with her husband-to-be and had enjoyed sex with him. The moment they were married she became frigid and unable to enjoy such intimacy any longer. As we talked it became obvious that Jane's problem lay in her mother's attitude to sex. She knew that her mother had disliked, even disapproved of sex. While she was unmarried her mother had not known that her daughter was having sex but now she was married she knew her mother would be aware that she was having sexual intercourse and be disapproving. The thought of her mother's disgust was ruining Jane's sex life.

Parents are often acutely embarrassed when their child first discovers his genitals and touches them in front of guests! The reaction is to put an immediate stop to the activity by shaming the child or surrounding the act with guilt. 'Don't be dirty,' or 'nice little girls don't touch themselves there'. Pleasure is immediately soured and the child is left with bad feelings about an important part of himself. Everyone said nice things about his eyes, his dimples and his long legs — what on earth was wrong with his penis?

Parents need to respond in a relaxed way to this new-found interest in the sexual organs. To accept it as normal is to convey the message that 'sex is good, and your sexuality is acceptable to us'. However, the child needs to know that some things are better not done in public!

The marriage is safe

It is vital that the child who flirts with the opposite-sex parent should lose the contest. Problems arise when the parents do not have a good sex life and their needs are not being met within the marriage. Sometimes the child does not have to try very hard to win Mummy or Daddy. Some parents too readily start meeting their needs in their children. Such needs may be either sexual or emotional. Emotional incest occurs when there is a lack of emotional and physical intimacy within the marriage relationship and a parent turns to a child of the opposite sex for companionship and comfort. Emotional incest can be just as damaging as physical incest. The most important but simple need for every child is to have parents who love each other and can show this unashamedly in the presence of their children.

The third stage is safely negotiated once a child has found the parent's marriage to be safe, has failed to win the desired parent and has decided that if he can't beat them it's best to join them. So a boy will identify himself with his father, admiring him and copying him and deciding to find a mate one day like his mother. In the same way a girl will identify with her mother, modelling herself on her, and deciding to choose a partner like her father − one day!

For many people this stage in their sexual development is not negotiated smoothly. Such adults are sexually inhibited and embarrassed as a result. Others battle with consequences that seem out of control. Unresolved difficulties encountered in this stage manifest themselves later in various ways. For some people the resulting problem may be fairly unimportant though still hard to overcome. For example, one result may be the need to make love in the dark, which, providing the partner does not mind, is not too disastrous. However, for others the consequences may be extremely hard to live with, as in the case of a young man I heard speak recently who had struggled for many years with a homosexual problem. His neurosis had its roots in a childhood spent trying on the one hand to look after his mother and on the other to avoid his abusive father. He never separated from his mother or crossed over to his father's side. His sexual identity had never been properly developed.

The consequences of failure to negotiate the third stage

Fear of success

A child who comes near to winning the flirtation with mother or father dangerously undermines his own security. Fear of success, a consequent loss of potency and lack of achievement could result. It is hard for a child to control his own impulses at this age and the fear of their power to destroy his security may cause him to inhibit or over-control them. It is as if the brakes are put on the natural sexual responses and kept on even when the danger has passed. 'The prospect of breaking his parents' marriage up is so frightening that he will become scared of his developing sexual awareness – which seems to be causing all these problems. So he may, so to speak, cut the telephone wires between his brain and his sexual feelings, leading to frigidity or impotence in adulthood.'[5]

Fear of success may also take the form of being attracted only to an unattainable person. The moment that person becomes available the fear surfaces and the attraction wanes.

Fear of punishment

Other fears may accompany the danger of winning or nearly winning a parent's exclusive love. Feelings of guilt and fear of punishment may surface whenever any relationship is formed with the opposite sex, however innocent.

Incest, whether this takes place with physical intimacy or through emotional closeness and dependency, means in effect that the child has won the contest and will consequently suffer hatred and jealousy from the ousted parent. One lady confessed to me that she had felt guilty for her parents' divorce for thirty years. She never knew the 'root' of it all until the Holy Spirit showed her very clearly that emotional incest was the cause of her guilt feelings. She was the only daughter (with four brothers) and was most definitely her 'Daddy's little princess' all her life. She could never understand why her mother was so jealous of her.

Most women who have been victims of incest with their father have felt their mother disliked them, even where the mother was apparently ignorant of what was happening. The daughter, nevertheless, saw herself as a rival to her mother and sensed her jealousy and mistrust.

Fear of a jealous rival may haunt any subsequent relationships. I remember one such young girl expressing a fear of making her counsellor's wife jealous even though she was never alone with him and only after she was given the opportunity of talking to his wife were her fears calmed.

Inhibition of normal sexual feelings

Guilt, shame, disgust and fear can all turn off normal sexual feelings. Men who were victims of intimacy with a needy mother during this stage may not have a homosexual problem so much as a problem with women. Their instinct for survival will come to the fore at the hint of a relationship with the opposite sex becoming more than platonic. This instinct protects them from ever again being engulfed by a woman.

Parents who show dislike and embarrassment over sex leave the child an inheritance of nasty feelings. Either extreme prudishness, inhibitions or frigidity may result. We laugh at the Victorian bride living in a far-flung part of the British Empire who asked her mother what she should do on her wedding night. 'Shut your eyes and think of England,' was the only advice she received. Yet how many women still close their eyes and think of tomorrow's lunch!?

We counsel many women who have inhibited their husbands from approaching them sexually by the time they reach middle age. Some even earlier. Sex for these women has always been an unwelcome experience. Once the family has arrived they have come to regard sex as an unnecessary extra. Usually these women are frigid and unable to respond with any feelings of pleasure. It is as if the normal sexual responses have been disconnected. Incest in childhood may also cause this lack of feeling in the sexual organs. Suppression of feelings was the only way of coping with the original violation and an early 'switch off' is difficult to reverse later.

Sexual neurosis

A severe sexual neurosis usually has its roots in an earlier stage. However, this third stage will either establish it or diminish it. If the parents change in their behaviour and attitude to the child the previous harm may be reversed.

Transsexual behaviour is usually rooted back at the stage a boy should be transferring from his mother's side to join his father. If there is no father figure and the mother encourages the son to stay close to her he will find extreme difficulty in making the necessary transition over to the man's side. He isn't even aware of the possibility until too late. Confusion over sexual identity may result. He may feel like a girl but in fact be a boy. No healing will come until the young man is finally 'divorced' from his mother.

A finding common to transsexualism, transvestism, homosexuality (in both sexes), exhibitionism, indecent exposure, impotence and many other sexual disorders is the over-possessive engulfing mother together with a weak or absent, or sometimes harsh and distant (but in either case unloving and unavailable) father, both of whom have a bad relationship as a couple and with one of whom the child is encouraged to side.[6]

A homosexual problem may be the result of too close an affinity with mother and too little identification with father. 'A mother, overly protective and peculiarly or injuriously intimate with a son — unless a strong and affirming father figure is close at hand — can render a son unable to separate his sexual identity from hers, and she thereby becomes part of any propensity toward homosexual behaviour that might crop up in him.'[7] Perhaps father was too weak, or too busy to encourage and beckon his son over to his side. The boy is then left longing for intimacy and identification with his father but unable to make the transition without help. Nor has his masculinity been affirmed or called forth by his father. He is stuck therefore in his sexual development at the point of transition.

The woman with a lesbian tendency may still be waiting to be embraced by a mother who could not achieve the intimate bonding every baby needs. Or maybe the separation came too soon and the baby was left with an aching need to nestle once again in her mother's arms. I recently talked with a young woman who had been a lesbian. She told me her mother had died when she was very small and her father had been left to bring her up. She survived living with her unaffectionate father by becoming a 'little tough guy'. However, her need to be cuddled and held by her mother surfaced in her teens when she became attracted to other girls. Gradually these relationships developed into sexual ones as she sought to meet her deep need for mother-love.

Conversely, lesbian behaviour could express the need to be free from the domination of a possessive mother. A girl may reject her mother in an effort to become disentangled from her possessive embrace and in so doing reject her own femininity. She may then proceed to look for it in other women. Leanne Payne writes of the 'cannibal compulsion' in the homosexual. 'Homosexual activity is often merely the twisted way a person tries to take into himself — in the mistaken way of the cannibal — those attributes of his own personality from which he is estranged.'[8] This is in reality a form of self-love or narcissism.

Recently I heard a formerly practising homosexual tell how he had been healed of his sexual neurosis. He described the homosexual as a person who had become stuck in his or her emotional growth. The healing, he explained, came as he was helped by loving friends to work through the process of growth to maturity. The healing of sexual dysfunctions, which arise out of problems in this third stage of development, is possible, though it will take time, God's grace, and the love and patience of understanding friends.

When successfully negotiated, this stage will have laid an important foundation for sexual functioning in later life. For now we must leave behind the messy glories of the nursery and pick up our story again amidst lunch-boxes, roller-skates, reading, writing and arithmetic. School-days have arrived.

Exercises

1. In your journal describe how you perceived your parents' attitude to sex and how you see that as affecting you.

2. Write a letter (not to be sent) first to your mother and then to your father (even if they are deceased). Tell them about the relationship you had with them in your childhood. How you viewed each of them, the place they had in your life and the experiences you had together.

Face up to the failure (if that is the truth) of your parents to help you develop a healthy attitude towards your own sexuality and to sex in general.

3. Write another letter to them (again not to be sent) forgiving them for any way in which they may have damaged your sexuality. Where incest, either emotional or physical, was the problem you may need help to face up to, and work through, all the varied emotions caused by such a violation – anger, guilt, hurt and the pain of a lost childhood.

4. Before you ask God to reach back into the past for healing, you may need to ask His forgiveness for any wrong behaviour or wrong attitudes, and His help in changing them. Even if they were caused by others in the beginning the responsibility for dealing with them now belongs to you.

5. If you are suffering from any sort of sexual neurosis pray through this with your friend/counsellor. Go back in your

prayer to where you now see you became stuck in your sexual development. Try in your imagination to take the developmental step you have never properly taken.

For example:

a) You may realise that you have never properly separated from your mother and crossed over to your father's side, becoming identified with his masculinity. Visualise yourself at the age of three or four and in your imagination take a step away from your mother and over to your father's side now. Where there has been an absent or weak father figure it may help you to visualise men you know and admire as good husbands and fathers. Now step across the line and identify with them. Ask Jesus to help you make the transition and affirm your sexuality. You may need to retake this step in prayer many times.

OR

b) You may be a woman who has never felt really feminine and is attracted to other women. In your imagination go back to the age of three or four. Line your family up on either side of a path. Place the women on one side and the men on the other. Where do you fit? Start accepting the little girl God made you and take some steps towards the female side. You may not like it at first but ask Jesus to show you how He sees you and ask Him to affirm you in your sexual identity.

6. Be involved, as much as possible, with older couples in the church who you know will affirm you as a person. If you can, share with them your need to have your femininity or your masculinity affirmed.

7. Use your two-way journal often and ask God to speak to you with regard to your sexuality, to affirm you as a person, to heal your emotions and to renew you in the attitude of your mind.

8. WIDENING HORIZONS
(Fourth stage, 6–12 years)

'Then the whining School-boy with his satchel
And shining morning face, creeping like snail
Unwillingly to school.' William Shakespeare[1]

We have examined the three foundational stages of a child's early development but it would be wrong to suggest that a child's personality has now been decided. 'For the child is not finished at six; his personality is not fixed or frozen into permanent form.'[2] The early experiences will have provided the foundations on which the personality will develop but no one can predict in which way these experiences will affect or influence this development. Every baby born is totally unique and completely different from any other person. He will react to his life situations in his own individual way. It is always fascinating to hear two people recount their memories of the same childhood experience and to realise how different their reactions to it were.

Our reactions to early experiences may all be different but for each of us the first six years are vital to personality formation. In the years to come many other influences will affect our ongoing development. A teacher, a family friend, or a neighbouring family may have a great influence upon our lives. In fact, after the age of six, outside influences play an increasingly important part. Nevertheless a secure home base with healthy family ties will be the best launching pad for entering this busy fourth stage.

Good foundations and bonding to parents increase the

capacity for tackling the challenges, opportunities, difficulties and problems that will occur during the years of six to twelve. Such foundations and bonding will not secure a problem-free life or be a complete insurance against developing a mental or emotional illness of some sort. But evidence indicates that attachment to a secure home base enhances the capacity for dealing appropriately with problems as they arise.

> It appears that parents need not be paragons; they may be inexperienced, they may be permitted to err in the fashion of the species, to employ sometimes a wrong method or an unendorsed technique, and still have a good chance of rearing a healthy child if the bonds between parents and child are strong and provide the incentives for growth and development in the child. [3]

Though the studies done of individuals 'who it is reasonable to believe possess well-functioning and healthy personalities' are not totally adequate their findings are very suggestive. 'So far as it goes, each study gives the same picture; the picture of a stable family base from which first the child, then the adolescent and finally the young adult moves out in a series of ever-lengthening excursions. Whilst autonomy is evidently encouraged in such families, it is not forced. Each step follows the previous one in a series of easy stages. Though home ties may be attenuated they are never broken.'[4]

So family ties and attachments will continue to be important as horizons widen and the child tackles the next stage in his development.

The tasks of the child in the fourth stage

Academic and social activity

The issue in this stage is one of Industry versus Inferiority.

It is certainly a period marked by activity rather than passivity. Energy is directed towards academic and social activity. Teachers and friends become the main topic of conversation. Important lessons in sharing, taking turns, losing and winning are being learned alongside the academic lessons. It is the age of questioning. The words 'why?' 'how?' 'when?' and 'what for?' are repeated so frequently that parents wonder if they are in danger of losing their reason while the child is gaining his!

New models

Outside influences will increasingly provide the child with different models to internalise, enlarging and enhancing his world view. It is often at this stage that a child from a dysfunctional family will have his first introduction to normal family life. Without any show of emotion a middle-aged man told us the story of his grey, cold childhood. It was only as he remembered visiting a neighbour's home that he broke down and wept. The love, warmth and laughter he had witnessed there left a lasting impression upon him. Very often these new models are held within a child and in later years brought out and used both positively and negatively.

One outside influence in my childhood stands out in my memory. My own father was so introverted and quiet that any conversation with him was usually monosyllabic. But when I was ten I met Frank who was to have a lasting influence upon my life. Frank was paralysed completely and was one of my sister's patients. He came to stay with us on several occasions and during these stays I rarely left his side. He was the most interesting person I had ever met. He spoke five different languages and from his imprisoned position he opened up a new world for me. His courage and vitality inspired me and Richard Lovelace's well-known words 'Stone walls do not a prison make, Nor iron bars a cage,' were proved to be true to me.[5] I realised that the human spirit could be free even within a paralysed body. At that time I was still a grubby tomboy and yet Frank always treated me with gentleness and consideration, listening and talking to me for hours on end. He gave me the feeling that maybe one day I could become the person of value he perceived me to be.

The internal policeman

Away from parental control the child is put in a position of having to exert some form of self-control. His conscience is becoming increasingly alive and acts as an internal policeman. This prevents a child doing certain forbidden things or exerts pressure, in the form of guilt, if he transgresses. 'Such a conscience does not emerge in the child until the fifth or sixth year. It will not become a stable part of his personality until the ninth or tenth year. It will not become completely independent of outside authority until the child becomes independent of his parents in the last phase of adolescence.'[6]

Although conscience is emerging, a desire to explore the exciting new world will inevitably mean the child oversteps the boundaries occasionally. My own mother was very strict over certain things and very easygoing over others. It was hard, at six, to get it right always and I clearly remember receiving a particularly painful punishment and telling myself, 'Now I know, I will never make that mistake again.' I was, in fact, making my own internal book of rules and becoming my own policeman.

Though parental discipline is an important factor in developing a good conscience and learning self-control, the example of consistent godliness on the part of the parent will in the long run exert a greater influence upon a child.

Christian parents sometimes fear the pressure on their children from the secular society in which they live and consequently are tempted to use spiritual blackmail to instil the strong conscience which they feel will protect them from evil. I was once present when a friend's son of eight was sent to his room to pray until he was convicted by God of his sin and had repented of some boyish misdemeanour. Instead of a good conscience, anger and rebellion will be the result of such spiritual pressure.

Sexual curiosity

Freud called this the latency stage and with regard to sexuality this is in part true. Sexual development is latent, though the interest is still there. Curiosity about the reproductive organs of the opposite sex continues and occasionally children will indulge in a form of sex play with one another. A few months ago I watched a television interview with a convicted child rapist. He was imprisoned for raping two little girls of between eight and ten years old. He told the story of his life in a children's home where he had been sent at the age of five. The only friend he ever had was a little girl of eight and together they experienced intimacy and affection by fondling and touching each other's sexual organs. At nine he tried to have intercourse with her and failed to get a full erection and she ended up by laughing at him. This experience left him with a compulsion to prove himself to little girls and a longing to recapture the only feelings of closeness and intimacy he had ever known.

Though few children will have had such an extremely damaging experience of sex, many between the ages of six and twelve will have indulged in sex play in some form. Much of this will be harmless and serve only to satisfy curiosity. The internalised policeman will normally act as a healthy controlling influence, though not every child is able to develop a good conscience as we saw in the above example. Certainly from that tragic history it emerges that he had not had a favourable environment in which to learn self-control. His childhood up until five was dominated by an abusive uncontrollable father from whom he was involuntarily removed when his mother went into hospital. From then on the only affection he experienced was of a sexual nature from a girl of eight. His lack of self control and his compulsion to be intimate with little girls was easily understood, though we can never excuse it. Now, as an adult, lacking his own internal policeman he had to be controlled by an external one and shut away in prison.

The parental task

Clearly a parent is still needed to aid in the development of self-control; to continue defining the boundaries; to set Christian standards and give an example of a godly life style. Other components are also important to a child's development at this stage.

Unconditional love and encouragement

This is a stage of industry and achievement. New skills are being acquired and the child needs the right balance between encouragement to work and statements of unconditional love. It is hard for any parent to put across the correct message at this stage. Other pressures often cause the child to interpret the message incorrectly. Encouragement to achieve may then be taken to mean, 'I am only loved if I do well.' Or a declaration of unconditional love may be interpreted as, 'They don't care about my work so there is no point in trying.'

The child needs constant encouragement and praise for all his efforts, successful or otherwise. However, love and affection should be shown consistently and be quite separate from achievement. Cuddles and hugs for no reason other than a demonstration of love separate the love from the achievement.

Letting go

When my oldest child went off to school for the first time, though I had my hands full with a new baby and a toddler, I felt bereft. I hovered in the classroom on the first day, reluctant to leave her. The German Fräulein in charge of the class shooed me out, commanding me to go home. I made my way to the end of the passage and turning the corner bumped into three other Mums hiding from the Fräulein, but not wanting to abandon their offspring. We seemed like a band of guilty conspirators in our common fear of finally 'letting go' to return to what seemed an empty house.

It is important for a mother to be definite and firm about school. The child needs to be left in no doubt that this is the next stage for them both. They may miss one another and look forward to being together again but the child needs mother's approval and help to enter with zest into this new phase.

Availability

When the last child leaves for school this is often mother's long awaited opportunity to regain her own independence and return to work. It is good for her to resume the outside activities that have been curtailed for so long. David has often told me how amazed he was at the effect upon me when our last child finally started going to school. He said the weight of years seemed to roll away and I looked ten years younger. However, the child has not ceased to need the security of mother's presence in the home. Arriving home from school in the afternoon was an important time for our children. Often the difficulties and problems would come tumbling out amidst tears and sobs. At other times a relaxed half an hour talking over the day's activities was all that was needed. But at times they would simply rush in and rush out again to play and I would wonder why I had hurried back so early to be available.

During one of our furloughs in England our oldest daughter attended a local school for the few months we were in the country. One afternoon she came running home from school looking white and shaken. She had just been subjected to her first lecture on sex, accompanied by a film. With obvious relief she sat down to tell me all about it. Half-way through she suddenly burst into tears. 'What about the children who don't have a Mummy at home?' she cried. She knew that several of her friends returned home every day to empty houses.

In whatever way a mother organises her new-found freedom availability to listen to and communicate with the children at their most obvious times of need should be a top priority.

Communication of feelings

Communication is the foundation stone in any relationship. Good communication takes place on all levels. From the cliché level, to reporting facts, sharing opinions and ideas, sharing feelings and on to total honesty and openness (see Chap. 1). A school-aged child will begin to curtail his conversation and only communicate on the first two levels if for any reason the other levels are discouraged. If opinions are laughed at, or never taken seriously, the child will soon learn not to share them. If feelings are handled badly, or not accepted as normal, a child will soon learn the art of suppression.

Most parents live with the false notion that a child must be protected from sadness. Coming back from boarding school one holiday I was hurt to find my pet budgerigar,

Peter, would not come onto my hand. On closer inspection I discovered he was not Peter at all. Trying to shield me from the grief of Peter's death my parents had gone to the trouble of buying an exact replica in the hope I would not notice the difference. Grief, sadness, loss, are all part of life and a child needs to learn how to handle these difficult emotions in a healthy way by expressing and feeling them within the family. 'The family that feels together heals together' was a wise comment I heard recently.

Selma Fraiberg tells the moving story of a little boy who was unable to cry and reacted to loss and separation from loved ones with 'inscrutable indifference'. He often spoke of a much-loved grandfather but could not remember his grandfather's death when he was five. Apparently the grandfather's death had been a great calamity in the family but the mother, who was most affected, was determined to keep up a brave front with the children. She never cried or grieved in their presence. She contained her feelings and the little boy learned to contain his. Unfortunately he paid a price for his apparent indifference to loss and frequently suffered allergic symptoms. 'His suppressed longing to cry could only be satisfied by the symptomatic weeping that accompanied his allergy.'[7]

Appropriate expression of feelings should be modelled by parents as well as taught. However, 'the right to have a feeling is not the same as a license to inflict it on others'.[8] Anger is a normal feeling to have on occasions and a person who has no anger available may feel very unprotected. We worked for a time with a young woman who had a great fear of men as a result of being incestuously molested when small. She apparently never experienced anger and without it was particularly vulnerable to attack. We talked and prayed through this on many occasions until the feeling became available to her; with it she felt more able to protect herself and her fear of men began to abate.

Anger, however, for a child is a difficult feeling to handle and it can be very frightening to feel out of control. Limits should be placed on the expression of anger. A child may have every right to feel angry, to say so and to show it, but does not have the right to strike those he is angry with or verbally abuse them. Self-control and the appropriate expression of feelings is an important lesson to be learned from parents. St Paul put it well: 'In your anger do not sin' (Eph.4:26).

Encouraging spiritual autonomy.

Up until this point a child will probably have accepted the faith of his parents without too many questions. Now he has reached the stage when he must begin to find his own faith. Just as the stage of autonomy, both physical and emotional, is negotiated only gradually, so too will spiritual autonomy be reached slowly.

Peer pressure as well as parental failures are bound to cause some difficulties to a child on the road towards faith. Christian friends and a lively church group will encourage a child to continue in his church attendance and his personal pilgrimage at this time. As a child comes towards his teens it is worth crossing all denominational barriers to find a lively church that caters for young people.

Another reason for a growing indifference to Christian things may be the failure of parents to spend quality time with their children. One man gave as the reason for his adult children turning away from the Christian faith, his failure to spend time with them when they were growing up. Instead he had been engrossed in a Christian ministry that took all his attention. Children need to rebel and flex their muscles as they prepare themselves for independence. However, their rebellion will be within normal limits if they are not already suffering anger and resentment against an absent parent whose absence is due to the demands of God and His church.

Encouraging co-operation and self-responsibility

From six to twelve a child needs to take on more and more responsibility for his own life. For a parent to be continually at a child's beck and call is not giving him the opportunity to feel his own weight. At six and seven a child needs to be reminded to take his gym shoes to school on the right day; by twelve he should be remembering for himself and taking the consequences if he forgets.

Co-operation with the other members of the family and taking responsibility for certain tasks is good preparation for the greater responsibility of the adolescent.

Difficulties arising from failure in this stage

A sense of failure

A man of forty confessed to us his total lack of confidence in his capacity to provide for his family and succeed in his job. He felt himself to be a failure at everything he attempted, though this was not in any way a true assessment of his life. We soon discovered that while he was growing up he could not remember his father ever giving him a single word of encouragement. He always seemed to have been at pains to put him down and to point out his shortcomings. Failure had haunted his childhood and was part of his normality. Though his father was no longer there to draw attention to his failures he was unable to shut out the critical parental voice. He had in fact taken up where his father had left off and continued the condemnation against himself.

False guilt and shame

At the end of a morning's lecture in Western Australia a young woman came up to me and said that she understood for the first time why she always felt so guilty. I had mentioned the fact that often parents are disappointed in their children for one reason or another. Perhaps they were expecting a boy and got a girl! Or wanted an athlete to carry on the family tradition and got an academic instead. Consequently a child may carry guilt for not being what was wanted. This young woman realised that she had always felt guilty for not being a boy who could one day take over the family farm.

Parents can put false expectations upon a child, maybe even seek to live vicariously through a child, trying to satisfy some frustrated ambition of their own. The child struggles to be what is desired but constantly fails and feels condemned and guilty.

Another reason for a sense of guilt and self-condemnation is 'shaming'. Parents may have used shaming as a way of controlling a child. The words 'you are a disgusting child' can pierce like a sharp sword into the child's soul and be hard to eradicate. It is painful to be alongside an adult who has felt again the pain of those words said years before. How often have I heard the sobs of agonising shame: 'I'm disgusting, I'm disgusting', as counsellees take upon themselves their parents' judgement against them.

> Shame is the uncomfortable or painful feeling that we experience when we realise that a part of us is defective, bad, incomplete, rotten, phoney, inadequate or a failure. In contrast to guilt, where we feel bad from doing something wrong, we feel shame from being something wrong or bad. Thus guilt seems to be correctable or forgivable, whereas there seems to be no way out of shame. [9]

Fear of loss or separation

It is in this fourth stage of development between the ages

of six and twelve, that some parents decide to send their children away from the protection and influence of home to be educated in a boarding school. My own experience of boarding school was a happy one but it separated me at an early age from my parents and I never had any real communication with them after that time.

'Involuntary separation and loss are potentially traumatic over many years of infancy, childhood, and adolescence.'[10] My oldest daughter was left at boarding school in England at the age of fourteen, while we went back to Chile with the rest of the family. For her it was the most traumatic time of her life. However well she understood her educational needs and could rationalise the situation we were in, the separation from us was almost unbearable. During one vacation she told us the sad story of another missionary family who were at the same school. These two children had been separated from their parents since the age of six and were in their teens when Charlotte met them. One Saturday she was asked to go and find these two because their parents had arrived back in England on a surprise visit and of course wanted to see their children. Charlotte found them eventually in the art room. Excitedly she told them the good news. 'Your parents have come.' Neither child moved – did not even glance up from their work. After a pause one of them mumbled to Charlotte in an unemotional voice. 'And who cares anyway?' They seemed dead to the most vital relationship a human being can have.

Involuntary separation can create a fear of making close relationships. Normal attachment behaviour is then blocked and cold, distant relationships are all that is possible.

Sexual problems

We have already cited the case of the child rapist whose only experience of intimacy and affection between the ages of five and ten had been of a sexual nature. Though sexual curiosity is natural, continued sexual intimacy of any kind within a family or outside will not only leave a child feeling defiled and with a great sense of guilt and self-loathing, it can also damage a child's sexual orientation for later in life.

One young woman carried guilt and shame for years as a result of sex play with an older brother. She felt unable to express her own sexuality and was ashamed of many of her womanly attributes. However, she was unable to totally suppress her sexual feelings and was continually plagued with the desire to masturbate.

An over- or under-developed policeman

Conscience is being developed gradually during this period and the parental rules and regulations are being slowly digested and internalised. Over-strict parenting with too many rules may result later in an over-developed internal policeman who controls with silly rules and then condemns a person for failing to keep them completely.

An under-developed internal policeman may be a problem for some adults. They may always be in trouble without feeling any stabs of conscience. Possibly the parents were constantly nagging and the child blocked out the voices and ceased to listen. Or perhaps ridiculous rules made him rebellious and angry and he paid the parents back with his bad behaviour. Another reason for an undeveloped conscience could be lack of good boundaries when growing up, leaving a child not knowing where the limits are.

Anger and resentment towards God

A young woman, born in Africa of missionary parents, sat in our counselling room and expressed bitter anger at God for His unfairness towards her. She told us a sad story of Christian parents and other significant adults who had treated her carelessly and thoughtlessly when she was growing up. Her self-worth had been whittled away leaving her with resentment and bitterness, not towards her Christian parents, but towards the God who had dominated all their lives.

In fact this young woman's anger should properly have been directed towards her parents and the church. It is no fault of God that people, to whom He has entrusted the care of children, fail through selfishness and pride. Once anger is owned and aimed towards the correct target there is a chance that forgiveness can be released and the festering wound can be cleansed and healed.

The memories during this period of childhood are readily available for recall and may therefore appear easier to deal with. Also because it is an age of reason and understanding it may be easier to rationalise the trauma away and deal with it superficially.

In fact the hurts may have cut very deep and take more than just one prayer to work through, as in the case of a teenager who yet again broke down and wept over a father who had continually shamed him and despised him. 'When will it stop?' was his cry. The pain seemed to be unending. The deprivation of a good-enough parent must be grieved. Like a bereavement it has to be worked through. One day it will be over for this teenager and he will come into a place of peace. Sadness may always be there but forgiveness and healing should eventually take the place of anger and hurt. So be patient and take time as you work through the following suggestions and prayers.

Exercises

1. Read the following questions and where the answer is in the affirmative write it in your journal in the form of a statement.

For example. If you answer 'yes' to 'Do you fear becoming attached to someone?' write down 'I am afraid of becoming attached to another person'.

Do you often feel condemned and guilty?

Do you often feel a failure?

Do you often feel embarrassed and ashamed?

Do you fear being alone?

Do you fear becoming attached to someone?

Do you overly express your feelings?

Do you always suppress your feelings?

Do you have any sexual problems?

Do you feel angry with God?

2. With your friend/counsellor ask God to bring to your mind any situation, relationship or experience that could have contributed to the problem you have just stated.

3. Take time to remember the situation, relationship or experience and describe it fully to God either aloud or in your diary. As you describe the memory be aware of the feelings that the memory evokes and describe them too.

4. Ask God to give you fresh insight about yourself, the other person or persons, the situation or the experience.

Ask God to show you what steps He wants you to take in order to resolve the problem.

5. Having done this give God time to minister His healing to you. Go back in your mind to the situation and ask Jesus to come into it. Wait for Him to make His presence known to you.

What is He doing?

Is He saying anything to you?

When you are ready record what you have just experienced fully in your journal.

6. Spend time meditating on the following verses:

'The Spirit of the Sovereign Lord is on me, because the Lord

has anointed me to preach good news to the poor. He has
sent me to bind up the broken-hearted, to proclaim freedom
for the captives and release from darkness for the prisoners,
to proclaim the year of the Lord's favour and the day of
vengeance of our God, to comfort all who mourn, and
provide for those who grieve in Zion — to bestow on them
a crown of beauty instead of ashes, the oil of gladness
instead of mourning, and a garment of praise instead of a
spirit of despair' (Isa.61:1–3).
OR

7. Take a journey with Jesus through Psalm 23. Take a verse
at a time and apply it to a specific painful memory of your
childhood. (This is best done in the presence of your friend
or counsellor. Though it is not his comfort that you need,
only his support.)
For example: v.4. 'Even though I walk through the valley
of the shadow of death, I will fear no evil, for you are with
me; your rod and your staff they comfort me.'

Perhaps you can remember a time of great fear in your
childhood when you felt overwhelmed and desperately
alone. First ask Jesus to be your Shepherd and accompany
you on your journey through this valley. Now in your mind
go back to the experience and holding tight to the hand of
Jesus walk through every part of it. As the feelings surface
cry out to Him and tell Him all about it. Then allow Him
to comfort you.

8. Continue to open this part of your life to God for His
full healing and until you see the changes begin to happen.
Keep praising and thanking God that He desires to change
you into the likeness of Jesus. 'And we, who with unveiled
faces all reflect the Lord's glory, are being transformed into
his likeness with ever-increasing glory, which comes from
the Lord, who is the Spirit' (2 Cor.3:18).

9. THE AGE OF CHANGE
(Fifth stage, Adolescence)

'There is only one cure for immaturity and that is
the passage of time.' Winnicott in Madeleine Davis
and David Wallbridge[1]

One school holidays, when I was going through the
uncomfortable period of adolescence, a friend announced
that she was to have a fancy dress ball for her sixteenth
birthday and I was to be invited. I went home and began
to make plans for my outfit and awaited the arrival of the
invitation. Other friends received theirs but mine never
appeared. I waited anxiously for the postman every day, but
the letter did not come. Eventually I came to the conclusion
the invitation had got lost; they had forgotten to send one,
or worse still, she had decided not to invite me. I told no
one of my dilemma. In my mind the problem grew and grew.
I could not go without an invitation but nor could I ask for
one. I suffered in silence and the day of the party came and
went. I felt rejected, embarrassed and wanted to curl up and
die. My friend told me later she was surprised I had not come
to her party!

This experience typifies the confusing and turbulent period
of puberty. It is a metamorphic period for us all. We seemed
locked into a self-centred, self-conscious, confusing world.
Some of us became tongue-tied and blushed so profusely
when spoken to that we preferred not to be noticed at all.
Our bodies were all gangly. Some parts were too big and
other parts too small. These were the days when voices began

to break, spots appeared, hair became greasy. Nothing about us seemed right. If, like a caterpillar, we could have hidden in some cocoon until the whole process was over and simply emerged as a butterfly, we would have grasped at the opportunity with thankfulness. Without such an option we had to make our own form of cocoon and hide for the duration within ourselves, or within our group.

Negotiating this last stage of childhood can be like shooting the rapids in a canoe for both parents and teenager. At times it feels as though Niagara Falls must be just around the corner. Everything that happens seems to take on an exaggerated significance. Life is full of drama and intensity. Situations assume the proportions of life and death. When my invitation failed to arrive I wanted to die. To this day, nearly forty years on, I still remember the intensity of my feelings then.

Puberty is a time of emotional turbulence and may have left some of us with unresolved problems to this present time. Understanding the developmental issues of this stage may help us in resolving the problems that still remain.

The developmental issues for the adolescent

Hormonal changes

Dr James Dobson believes that parents and behavioural scientists have underestimated the impact of the biochemical changes occurring at puberty. 'We can see the effect of these hormones on the physical body, but something equally dynamic is occurring in the brain. How else can we explain why a happy, contented, cooperative twelve-year-old suddenly becomes a sullen, angry, depressed thirteen-year-old? Some authorities would contend that social pressure alone accounts for this transformation. I simply don't believe that'[2] says Dobson.

The mood swings of the adolescent become less perplexing in the light of these hormonal changes, as the girl becomes a woman and the boy becomes a man.

Peer pressure

A young boy of fourteen sat in our counselling room with his mother and father and complained that he was forced to go out with them on family outings. 'I want to be with my friends,' he said. 'The family is boring. My friends mean everything to me.' His parents looked dismayed. In fact he was not being deliberately cruel. He was stating a fact. At fourteen the peer group is all important. Its influence, during this period, far outweighs the influence of the family. After investigation Dr Dobson concludes 'that peer pressure is a far more dominant factor in shaping teenage behaviour than parental influence'.[3] The need to be 'in' with the group is vitally important to the adolescent. His value and self-worth are dependent on his acceptance or non-acceptance by the group.

Popularity is often won by athletic prowess or good looks and to be accepted by this elite group, or smiled upon by them, can make the day, or conversely to be ridiculed or rejected by them can make life unbearable. I remember asking one young man to tell me about his experience of adolescence. He grimaced visibly as he thought back. 'It was awful, I can't bear to think about it,' he replied.

Our peer group influences how we feel about ourselves and can enhance or hinder our self-acceptance.

Self-acceptance

This is to do with how we see ourselves and how we feel about ourselves. Adolescence is accompanied by agonies of self-doubt and at times self-hatred. It is a journey out of which we should eventually emerge feeling reasonably secure and at peace with ourselves. 'The step of self-acceptance ideally comes just after puberty. Puberty/adolescence is the narcissistic stage for all of us. While in it, we are overly concerned and self-conscious about ourselves (especially our bodies) . . . whether or not we are acceptable to others or to ourselves.'[4] It is a painful time and so many things can hinder the process. A vital factor seems to be the acceptance or non-acceptance of our peers.

It is during this period that some young people become obsessed with their weight. They imagine themselves to be too fat and start dieting vigorously. Helena Wilkinson, a survivor of anorexia nervosa, tells the story of her struggle to survive this in her book *Puppet on a String*. She writes, 'The search for my own identity and difficulties over relationships were the two main features . . . and I believe they both played an important part in my developing anorexia.'[5] Many teenagers begin dieting seriously to enhance their looks which is quite common. But for it to become the obsessive disease of anorexia Helena believes there has to be an underlying problem of unmet emotional needs.

During adolescence there are various and simultaneous struggles overlapping and interlinked with one another; the struggle to belong, to be accepted, to be a person and prove one's sexual identity. Erikson suggests the main issue of this stage is 'Identity versus Confusion'. Winnicott says the problem of the adolescent centres around the statement 'I am' and the question, 'What am I?' Skynner points out that this stage is a re-run of earlier stages and the child struggles again with the issues of autonomy, attachment and sexual identity.

Sexual identity

This is linked closely with self-acceptance and may also be affected by peer pressure but the major influence on the emerging sexual identity will come from the father figure. His presence and affirmation is vital to both sexes.

With the hormonal activity sexual interest is stirred up again, this time much more powerfully. Once more the powers of attraction will be tried out on the opposite-sex parent but this time there is a difference. The adolescent is becoming sexually attractive and is experiencing real sexual feelings. This puts the parent in the hot seat.

As the teenager becomes more certain of his sexual identity flirting with those of his own age group will begin in earnest. However, most adults can remember having some ambivalent sexual feelings, if only for a short duration. Love and admiration for someone of the same sex were experienced, while at the same time an interest in the opposite sex was developing. 'Here again there is uncertainty, because in early adolescence "the boy or girl does not yet know whether he or she will be homosexual, heterosexual or simply narcissistic".'[6]

Remembering the 'crushes' that were so prevalent in my all-girls boarding school and the lack of opportunity for opposite-sex relationships, we were glad to send our own four girls to mixed schools. They entered easily into heterosexual relationships and enjoyed same-sex friendships without too much confusion. However, most people in their early teens will have experienced a passing attraction for a member of the same sex. Providing a good foundation was laid in the early stages and nothing happens during puberty to block the normal maturation process this homosexual stage will pass and a full heterosexual identity will be achieved.

Independence or self-reliance

In the journey through adolescence a child goes from dependence to independence. In the same way that a butterfly has to struggle to come out of the chrysalis, so does the teenager have to struggle to break loose from the safe, cosy environment of the family and try out his developing wings. The struggle is frequently accompanied by rebellion and anger at what the adolescent perceives as confining boundaries placed there by his parents. The need to break away from parental control is normal and feelings of frustration and anger with them enable the teenager to begin the necessary steps toward self-reliance and independence. In order to dissolve the intensity of the relationship and begin to move away, a child in a metaphorical sense has to be prepared to 'kill off' his parents. 'Winnicott deliberately used such evocative imagery when he wrote: ''If the child is to become an adult then this move is achieved over the dead body of an adult . . . where there is the challenge of a growing boy or girl, there let an adult meet the challenge. And it will not necessarily be nice.'' It is also necessary for an adult to survive this challenge, to be ''killed off'' and yet to rise again.'[7]

Struggle, pain, doubt, confrontation, anxiety are emotive words but can easily be used in connection with this stage. The process of maturation takes time and cannot be hurried. For both parents and adolescent it may be a 'long day's night'! However, if a parent is brave and strong enough to go through this painful process with his child and see him come out the other end, an adult to adult relationship can be built based on mutual respect.

The adolescent needs to achieve self-acceptance, a sexual identity and self-reliance. Then he is ready for independence. To achieve this he needs his parents' help.

The parental task

To stand firm

My oldest daughter, then thirteen, returned one evening from a Chilean friend's house in a very thoughtful mood.

'Maria says her parents don't love her,' she announced. 'Whatever makes her think that?' I asked. 'She says they don't care where she goes or when she comes in,' Charlotte replied. I knew that was true but I was amazed that Maria had put such a perceptive interpretation upon her parents' carelessness.

Even a rebellious, angry teenager still needs to be loved and to know that he is valued by his parents. He also needs to have something to struggle and push against like the butterfly emerging from the rigid chrysalis. So a parent needs to stand firm and keep defining the boundaries and limits. However, it is never wise to fight over non-essentials. A friend of mine recently had words with her father-in-law who kept nagging her teenage son to change his clothes. 'I don't like the way he dresses,' he explained. 'Well, we don't mind,' was her reply, 'so will you please leave him alone.' Actually I knew my friend wasn't that keen on her son's way of dressing either, but had decided it was not an essential issue.

It is a great temptation, especially for Christian parents, to put pressure on their children to conform so that they will not be embarrassed in front of their church friends. Some parents are idealistic and perfectionistic and James Dobson has a warning for those fathers and mothers 'who are determined to make their adolescents — all of them — perform and achieve and measure up to the highest standard. A perfectionist, by the way, is a person who takes great pains with what he does and then gives them to everyone else. In so doing, he rocks a boat that is already threatened by the rapids.'[8]

To give affirmation

Firmness coupled with acceptance of the adolescent as a person of value is the only antidote to the insecurities and agonising self-doubts that surround this age.

Leanne Payne emphasises again and again the crucial part

the father plays during this stage of development. 'The father's affirmation of his young one has been indispensable all along, of course, laying as it does the groundwork for a trusting relationship later on. But he must not opt out at this critical time in the life of the adolescent. The fact that the father's loving and affirming presence (or that of an extraordinary father substitute) is the ladder by which the young son or daughter takes this crucial developmental step up to self-acceptance has been impressed on me over and over again.'[9]

And again she writes:

> Both sexes listen for the masculine voice at puberty. Whether or not we come out of the narcissistic stage and accept ourselves depends upon the affirmation that comes from the masculine.
>
> When the father's strong hand of love and affirmation does not rest on his son's or daughter's shoulder, tragedy results, especially in this day of the diminished, nuclear family. Effective father substitutes are rare indeed. Grandfathers, uncles, and other masculine role models are even more remote than fathers.[10]

I would say that sixty per cent of all the people who come into our church counselling office seeking help have not been sufficiently affirmed by their fathers. This may not be the major problem in their life but it will have compounded their difficulties.

One young woman worked hard, over several months, dealing with problems resulting from her mother's apparent dislike and rejection of her. To begin with she insisted her problems were only caused by this bad relationship with her mother. However, her attention was gradually drawn to her weak and inadequate father. She could not remember him ever showing her overt affection or any kind of affirmation. On one occasion she broke down and wept bitterly, saying over and over, 'Dad I needed you so much, why weren't you there for me?'

It is a fact that many people who look to counsellors, doctors, or maybe even the church for help are really looking for that strong masculine affirmation that as toddlers and teenagers they did not receive. For a father to rejoice over his daughter's development into a woman is to reassure her and encourage her to become the woman God intended her to be. When a father spends time with his young son, cultivating common interests and talking with him, he is actually affirming his manhood.

To respect one another

With a teenager in the house tensions are bound to arise. These will be between mother and daughter, father and son, and often differences of opinion between the parents. It is important when this occurs that children know their parents love and respect one another and stand firmly together. If there is mutual respect then a good balancing act can be achieved. One parent may be too easy-going, while the other may be too strict and middle ground needs to be found. What often happens is that to balance the easy-going parent the other becomes more strict, and then the other tries to redress the balance by becoming more laid back. This results in polarisation instead of togetherness. Respect for one another's opinions will mean drawing nearer together instead of pulling apart. Consequently a greater degree of balance will be achieved.

To keep communicating

Silence and non-communication are the hall-marks of the adolescent. 'She doesn't tell me anything that's going on. If she did perhaps I could help,' complained the mother of a very unhappy teenage girl who was playing truant from school and bordering on anorexia. The only advice for such a mother is to be available and keep the lines of communication open.

It is important for a mother and daughter, as for a father and son, to spend time together. It is not too difficult to find a common interest; a football or rugby match, a TV programme to watch and talk about or an activity such as swimming. All my girls are what my husband David rudely calls 'sun worshippers' and will lie in the sun for hours. We have had some good chats lying in the garden undisturbed. Dobson believes that if a father and son can develop interests and hobbies together 'the rebellious years can pass in relative tranquillity.'[11]

To keep letting go

Parents often hang on to children longer than necessary or fail to prepare them for independence. One family I know actually put their children through a course on independence. They were taught how to manage their finances by father, to cook by mother. They went on journeys and had to use train timetables and work out the route. It was a deliberate policy of the parents to prepare their children for the future.

A teenager needs to begin feeling his own weight and start taking responsibility for his life and it is the parents' job to facilitate this.

It is especially important at this stage for parents to stop imposing their wishes regarding Christian activities. Providing there are other young people and the service and message are relevant, a teenager will most likely choose to attend church, but sooner or later the choice must be his.

It goes without saying that Christian values and standards cannot suddenly be imposed upon a teenager at this stage. If they have not been part of the early formative years it will be difficult to implement them now.

Conflict with an adolescent is bound to occur and the 'letting-go' process will often be fraught with problems. One of the greatest obstacles for a parent to overcome is his pride. Take the issue of dress, for example. Parents and teenagers frequently quarrel over this. The number of earrings in an ear, the hair style and colour, the clothes, or in some parent's eyes, the rags their child is wearing in public — in front of their friends, neighbours and other church members. If honestly examined, the pain for the parents is usually that they feel their once presentable and gifted son or daughter, their pride and joy, is letting them down and looking a mess!

To keep the home fires burning

Just as the mother's presence gave the toddler confidence to explore his environment, so will the security of home and the family give the adolescent courage to explore the wider world and try out his independence and self-reliance.

'The process of breaking out into ever widening circles is greatly facilitated by the continued existence of the family.' Even after independence has been fully achieved it is good to know home is still there and in its right place. At first the teenager experiments with independence. He may give it some trial runs. However, 'the excursion is only profitable if there is a return ticket'.[12]

When I wrote to my daughter at boarding school in England I would describe the house and the activities of the family in detail. She could then picture it all in her mind and have the security of knowing we were still there. One missionary family moved to another location while their daughter was away at boarding school. She became very unsettled, stopped communicating with the family and refused to visit them. She had lost her anchor. For an adolescent the family is his link with reality. Because they exist he exists; he belongs somewhere; he has roots. As his own sense of identity grows stronger he will need this reassurance less and less. However, the family ties and attachments continue to be important ingredients for emotional health and sense of well-being.

I began this chapter with the story of the fancy dress ball I never attended. One problem was my inability to communicate my dilemma to my parents. Another was my introverted feelings of self-doubt and self-consciousness. This is typical of the adolescent stage. None of us pass through this period totally unscathed. The wounds may have been superficial and easily healed with the passage of time. But some of the traumas of adolescence leave deep wounds from which we may not have fully recovered.

In each stage of development there are several important objectives to be reached. No less important are the developmental tasks of the teenager. As before, if these tasks are not adequately worked through, immature responses and behaviour patterns may result and pose difficulties for the next stage of life. Hence we have the young woman who leaves home to get married and finds she cannot cope without Mummy there to tell her what to do. The work of achieving self-reliance was not completed and will cause immature responses until worked through.

The unresolved problems of adolescence

Self-consciousness

Without having reached the place of self-acceptance, a person may be left in the narcissistic, self-absorbed place of the teenager. He or she may have difficulty looking outward toward others because of the painful feelings of embarrassment and self-consciousness. This person may have reached middle-age and still find it difficult to speak in a small group or be asked a question publicly. I recently chatted with a woman in her forties who still blushed and became tongue-tied whenever a man spoke to her. Her father had been a frightening, domineering man and had never affirmed her femininity. Consequently she was stuck in her emotional development and was unsure and embarrassed by her sexuality.

Masturbation

The narcissistic, self-absorbed stage of adolescence is part of a normal progression. It may be accompanied by the practice of masturbation. There are many forms of sexual perversion mentioned in the Bible but this is not included. However, this is a form of self-love, which if carried to excess or beyond the normal period of puberty, could become a distressing habit which is humiliating and hard to break. We all need to learn to be in control and not controlled by our sexual drives.

As Leanne Payne has observed, 'Masturbation is often a feature of puberty; as the narcissistic period lingers, so does the habit . . . In some instances, however, the habit is rooted in infantile trauma and is related to severe dread and anxiety — those components accompanying the severest psychological injuries in infants. In these cases, a dread-ridden masturbation (rather than a merely lustful one) ensues. The infant, unable to receive the love of the mother or someone other than himself, will anxiously clutch at his own genitals. Dr Frank Lake, Christian psychiatrist and depth-psychologist, states that infantile dread manifests itself as painful genital tension.'[13]

Although the Bible does not directly condemn masturbation, whenever it is practised compulsively to excess it causes self-disgust rather than self-acceptance. It is a wrong type of self-love which leads to self-hatred. We have ministered to many people with the habit, both married and unmarried. In all cases where it has been a compulsive habit, which is sometimes accompanied by sexual fantasies, the result has been guilt and self-loathing.

Introversion

During adolescence the friendly, out-going schoolgirl or boy changes into a self-centred, moody individual. A real identity crisis is in progress. 'Who am I?' 'Am I acceptable?' 'What do they think of me?' These questions and others like them fill the thought life. It may became morbid and unhealthy if carried on past adolescence. Leanne Payne calls this constant analysing and fragmenting of experience the 'disease of introspection'. It causes the sufferers to indulge in destructive and unedifying thought patterns about themselves and their experience of life. By questioning and analysing everyone and everything they destroy the spontaneous child-like self that responds naturally to God and others.

Eric was a well-educated, intelligent man in his thirties. He came for prayer suffering from various physical aches and pains and a constant nagging anxiety. The early sessions were dominated by long recitals of his thought processes and his analyses of himself. Hours of listening to tapes and reading books had aided his self-absorbtion. He was in fact suffering from the disease of introspection and fought every attempt to mend the split between his mind and heart. One key to solving his problem would have been to lay down the habit of analysing everything in his life and start feeling and experiencing life. Another key would have been to move, with the help of his counsellors, from the adolescent position of self-centredness to self-acceptance. Only then could he have been able to look outward and love others because then he would be loving himself in the true sense.

Sexual confusion

Adolescence is a progressive journey to a full secure

knowledge of one's sexual identity as a male or female. Some, however, get stuck in the homosexual phase of love towards the same sex. As with masturbation the cause of homosexuality may be much further back, rooted in infantile trauma. Or the cause may be right here in the teens. One young man admitted that he felt miserable as a teenager and looked with admiration and envy at the boys who were handsome and popular. His father was a nonentity in his life and had not been able to affirm his son's masculinity. Now fifteen years later this young man was stuck with the same adolescent feelings of attraction towards handsome, popular men of his own sex.

For many years I felt much more comfortable in jeans or a track suit. Having a normal heterosexual orientation and being happily married, it never occurred to me that I had never had my femininity affirmed or even called forth. As a child I had longed to be a boy and had even prayed to be changed into one. As God brought to mind some of the early traumas and the consequent vows I had made, I began to ask God to change the view I had of myself. As God affirmed my sexuality in a way my own father never had, I began to feel more and more comfortable being the woman He had meant me to be. The jeans went into the dustbin and my girls enjoyed helping me choose a new wardrobe. My husband became a happier man, even if a poorer one!

Sexual promiscuity

When freedom from an engulfing mother is not fully achieved, nor affirmation from an absent father received, an adolescent may be left with some sexual confusion. If, however, the teenager struggles hard and gains his freedom from the domination of mother, he or she is still left needing their sexuality to be affirmed by someone. This may lead them to try and prove their masculinity or femininity through conquests of the opposite sex. Compulsive flirting, even promiscuity, can then result.

Rebellion

Fiona, an attractive girl in her mid-twenties, was bewildered by her rebellious attitude towards men who attempted to give her any form of direction. As she described her childhood it became plain that she had never in fact freed herself from the control of her father. Though she no longer lived with him she felt his presence dominated her life. She would catch herself still trying to please him and live up to his expectations.

Rebellion is normal in a teenager struggling towards independence, but past the age when his independence should be firmly established, it points to some unresolved issues or unfinished business with parental or past authority figures.

Inadequacy

Lorna's mother had died the previous year and gradually she had become unable to cope with normal, everyday living. She felt inadequate, lonely and frightened by the responsibilities of life.

Alan was twenty-one and had moved away from home a year ago. Now he was back again with a string of unresolved problems and debts. He had wanted to be independent but had not yet acquired sufficient self-reliance to manage on his own.

There are many people like Lorna and Alan, who have never reached the place of self-reliance and independence. They live anxious lives always waiting for someone stronger to come and help them. Often they get married and become over-dependent, making the other partner into a parent. They produce children, rely upon them and succeed in making them into 'little adults' before their time. A friend of mine told me that from an early age her mother made her feel responsible. 'I was like the mother and she was like the child.' She felt as if her mother had stolen part of her childhood from her.

Inadequate people are usually the result of very authoritarian parents or an over-protected home-background. They have failed to negotiate the difficult adolescent journey from dependence through to independence and self-reliance.

The adolescent journey may be a long and arduous one, but it does eventually come to an end. Our first daughter was married at twenty. Our tiny premature baby had grown into a lovely young woman. Only a few years before we had been contending with a moody and rebellious teenager. Suddenly, almost from one day to another, the clouds had parted, the sun had come out and once more we had our happy, co-operative daughter back again. She had negotiated the rapids of adolescence and was ready to be launched as a fully fledged adult.

Most of us will have identified with areas of immaturity mentioned in this book. None of us will have made the journey through the various stages perfectly. At the beginning of this chapter I quoted Winnicott's statement that the only cure for immaturity was the passage of time. This is true in the process of normal growth, but where a person has failed to negotiate a developmental task at the appropriate stage the passage of time may only highlight the problem. The solution lies in going back to the task and with God's help renegotiating it. As He promised in Joel, He will repay us for the years the locusts have eaten (Joel 2:25). God is able to reparent us and make up that which has been lost or stolen from us. Our responsibility is to come into His presence and give Him the opportunity to address the need within us.

Exercises

1. What sort of relationship did you have with your earthly father? If you had no father then have in mind the most dominant male figure in your life. This may have been your grandfather, uncle or even a step-father. Ask yourself the following questions:

What experiences did we have together?

  Did he cuddle me?

  Did he spend time with me?

  Did he talk with me?

  Did he play with me?

  Did he pray with me?

  Did he protect me?

  Did he discipline me?

  Did he love me?

  Did he affirm me as a person?

  Did he affirm my sexuality?

How did I feel about him?

  Did I love him?

  Did I fear him?

  Did I miss him when he was away?

  Was I relieved when he was away?

  Did I feel safe with him?

  Did I respect him?

2. In your journal write a paragraph describing your teenage years. Express the real feelings surrounding those years and the relationship you had with your parents and in particular your father.

If you didn't feel accepted by him — then face that truth.

If you didn't have your sexuality affirmed — face the fact.

If you suffered agonies of embarrassment and self-consciousness — confront the reality of those bad feelings.

Grieve the loss of acceptance and affirmation. Forgive those who hurt you or were unavailable for you.

3. Find a quiet place and relax. In your imagination go to a favourite childhood spot. See Jesus coming towards you. Ask Him to sit beside you as you would have liked your father to have done.

Tell Him about those years, your fears, your worries, your pain and your hurt. Relax against Him and feel His masculine presence.

4. 'Ask and it will be given to you' (Luke 11:9). Ask your Heavenly Father to reparent you and help you take the steps up into a 'serene self-acceptance'. Use your two-way diary to make your request and then record God's response to your prayer.

God is a perfect Father and longs for us to know and experience His love and kindness. 'As God has said: "I will live with them and walk among them, and I will be their God, and they will be my people . . . I will be a Father to you, and you will be my sons and daughters, says the Lord Almighty".' (2 Cor.6:16,18).

5. Spend time meditating on the Fatherhood of God. Get to know the Father Heart of God. Floyd McClung has written a book with this title. In it he says, 'God is the Perfect Parent. He always disciplines in love. He is faithful, generous, kind, and just, and He longs to spend time with you. Your Father wants you to receive His love and to know that you are special and unique in His eyes.'[14]

6. Cultivate safe but intimate relationships within the Body of Christ. Learn to give and receive love and affirmation.

EPILOGUE

As parents we know the end of an era has come when we watch our son or daughter walk down the aisle on their wedding day. For us a new task will soon begin — that of being grandparents. But that is another story!

One by one our four daughters have left the protection of our home to start their own. We have loved them, cared for them, wept over them, fought with them and finally let them go. Now they are producing their own children and the whole cycle begins again.

However, were I to write the whole story of our girls' childhood and our attempts at parenting we could not pretend in any way to have been totally successful. On so many occasions and in so many situations we failed them, hurt them and caused them problems. My youngest daughter was listening to me talking to a small group of mothers with toddlers only this week and she told us afterwards how she had winced with pain when I had mentioned how often, when my children were small, my head had been buried in a book.

Some parents reading this book could be left with feelings of remorse. It has never been my aim to depress you or take you on a guilt trip. We may all have fallen short of our own standards in parenting, let alone God's, but God has not left us without hope. There is a remedy for the hurt that has been inflicted on us as well as the hurts we have inflicted on others. The answer lies in forgiveness: asking for it, receiving it and giving it.

Asking forgiveness from God

To recognise that we have sinned or failed to live up to a standard is the first step in dealing with that sin. It is good to be specific in naming our failures or our sins against others. It is only too easy to generalise and not face up to the pain of real incidents that we were actually responsible for. Sometimes our children suffered hurt which we caused even though we did not mean to hurt them and often did not know we had.

On one occasion in Chile one of my daughters was rushed into hospital for an emergency operation to remove her appendix. I was told I could visit her later that same day, but I was to ring first. Every time I rang the hospital the nurse said she could not be seen yet. Eventually it was too late and I had to wait until the next morning. When I arrived at the hospital I found a distraught child who had been waiting all night for me to come. The nurse had been putting me off for no good reason and I had not been demanding enough. I realised that I should not have taken that 'No' for an answer. I should have just turned up, if only for a good night kiss. Our daughter still remembers the incident and though I could have put the blame on to the nurse, in fact I caused the hurt and I was therefore responsible for asking both God and my daughter for forgiveness.

Asking forgiveness from our children

Once forgiveness has been asked for and received the door is open for God to come in and heal the hurt. The first step in the healing of our children may be when we, as parents, ask their forgiveness. When we ask for it, and they give it, the wheels are set in motion for the necessary emotional healing and restoration to take place.

Receiving forgiveness from God and our children

Remorse will only spiral us into condemnation and depression. Repentance leads to forgiveness and restoration. At some point we have to receive forgiveness from God and, when it is offered, from our children. The temptation, even after this, is to take out the big stick and punish ourselves for these many failures. We can so easily start blaming ourselves for all the problems our children have, even the ones that are not of our making. This is a dead end — with no through road. Maybe we need to start by asking why we need to use a big stick on ourselves and can't receive forgiveness as a free gift?

Giving forgiveness

Sometimes the hurt has been reciprocated. We have made mistakes and our angry child has hit back at us, wounding us deeply. In this case we will need to forgive him or her.

Releasing forgiveness has great power to heal. It can bring healing to our spirits, our emotions, our bodies and our relationships.

I remember being told the moving story of an elderly woman who was dying from cancer. Her son visited her in hospital and then went back home to tell his wife that his mother was dying and the doctors could do nothing more for her. On hearing this the wife suggested that her husband had some unfinished business with his mother that needed sorting out before she died. She then reminded him of a time when he was much younger and he had walked out of his home and had not been in touch with his mother for a whole year. 'You need to put that right with her before she dies,' said the wife. The son agreed and went back to the hospital and asked his mother to forgive him for his behaviour all those years ago. She was very moved and willingly forgave him and asked him to forgive her for causing him to be so unhappy that he felt he needed to leave home. They were completely reconciled and the son went home. The following week his mother was discharged from hospital completely well! She enjoyed good health for many more years and when she died later it was through the normal physical degeneration of old age.

There are many such stories of the restoring power of forgiveness. God seems to specialise in the restoration and re-making of broken relationships through forgiveness. A mother I know asked a married son to forgive her for hurting him with angry words when he was being a difficult teenager. He responded by hugging her and asking her to forgive him for being such a pain in the neck! Since then a new relationship has grown up which has given them both much pleasure and joy.

The healing of our children's hurts and the healing of our own hurts would happen naturally if asking for forgiveness, receiving and giving forgiveness could become a normal part of our family lives.

In Deuteronomy we read that Balaam son of Beor was hired to pronounce a curse on God's People but Moses reminded the Israelites how 'the Lord your God would not listen to Balaam but turned the curse into a blessing for you, because the Lord your God loves you' (Deut.23:5).

During our life time we have all been hurt and have inflicted hurt on others, but we have a God who can, in His gracious way, turn the curses into blessings because of His great love for His people.

STAGES OF DEVELOPMENT

	Issues for the Child	Issues for the Parent		Possible Result of Failure
		F	M	
In utero	Nurturing Basic trust	Recognition Welcome Bonding	Protection Support Bonding	Mistrust Inability to receive good from others or to feel good about oneself
Birth	Life	Hard work giving birth	Support Encouragement	Anger Speech difficulties Irrational fears Separation anxiety
1st Stage 0–12 months	Nurture Trust Internalising mother Beginning separation process	Nurturing through physical and emotional presence	Boundary maintenance Support	Mistrust of others Painful dependency needs Self-doubt or self-hate Depression
2nd Stage 15 months – 3 years	Initiative Independence Control Discovery Language Identity	Keeping boundaries Emotional security Stimulation Space Some gradual separation	Setting boundaries Stimulation Being different	Over-attachment to mother Attention-seeking Insecurity Rejection Lack of confidence

3rd Stage 3–6 years	Sexual identity Relationship to parents Interest in genitals Flirting with opposite-sex parent	Keeping the boundaries Marital relationship	Obsessive behaviour Rebellion Difficulty in relationships Fear of success Fear of punishment Inhibition of sexual feelings Sexual neurosis
4th Stage 6–12 years	Academic and social activity Outside influences Developing conscience Sexual curiosity	Unconditional love and acceptance Letting go Availability Communication of feelings Encouraging co-operation and self-responsibility	Sense of failure False guilt Fear of loss or separation Sexual problems Lack of self-control Anger or resentment
5th Stage Adolescence	Hormonal changes Peer pressure Self-acceptance Sexual identity Independence Self-reliance	Firmness Affirmation, especially from father Respect for one another Communication Letting go Keeping home fires burning	Self-consciousness Compulsive masturbation Introversion Sexual confusion Sexual promiscuity Rebellion Inadequacy

COUNSELLING SERVICES

British Assn of Counselling

1a Little Church Street
Rugby
Warwicks CW21 3AP

Care and Counsel

St Mary Magdalen Church
Holloway Road
London N87 8LT
Tel: 01-609 4545

Caring Professions Concern

The Kings Centre, High Street
Aldershot, Hants GU11 1DJ
Tel: 0252 317277

Centre for Christian Healing
Counselling and Training

Ellel Grange
c/o The Christian Trust
Cove Road, Silverdale
Carnforth, Lancs LA5 0SQ

Christian Listeners

Acorn Christian Healing Trust
Revd Anne Long
Stanstead Hall
Stanstead Abbots
Herts SG12 8AA

Clinical Theology Assn

Revd Peter van de Kasteele
St Mary's House,
Church Westcote
Oxford, Oxon OX7 6SF

Courses on Healing and
Deliverance

Revd Bill & Mrs Worboys
4 Berner Street
Felixstowe, Suffolk

C.W.R. Institutes of Christian Counselling	Waverley Abbey House Waverley Lane Farnham Surrey GU9 8EP
London Healing Mission	Revd Andy Arbuthnot 20 Dawson Place London W2 4JL Tel: 01-229 3349
North of England Christian Healing Trust	Spennithorne Hall Leyburn N Yorks DL8 5PR
Olive Branch Ministries (Midlands)	Revd Tom Gibson 16 Dorset Road Edgbaston Birmingham B17 8EN
Scargill House Marriage Review	Apply to Bookings Sec for information
Christian Growth and Gestalt Christian Counselling & Inner Healing	Scargill House, Kettlewell Skipton, N Yorks BD23 5HU
Church Army Counselling Centres	Independent Road Blackheath London SE3 9LG
Wholeness Through Christ	The Aministration Secretary 8 Beaulieu Way Swanwick, Derbys DE55 1DR
Network Counselling	10 Cotham Park, Cotham Bristol BS6 6BU Tel: 0272 420066

Especially for healing the homosexual

Mildmay Mission Hospital	Tel: 01-739 2331
Leanne Payne Restoring Personal Wholeness through Healing Prayer	c/o Personal Wholeness Conference 41c Dace Road London E2 2NG Tel: 01-986 7114
The Courage Trust	PO Box 338 Watford Herts WD1 1SJ Tel: 01- 428 3822
True Freedom Trust	Martin Hallett PO Box 3, Upton, Wirral Merseyside Tel: 051-503 07732
Turning Point	PO Box 572 London SE19 1EF Tel: 01-460 2425

RECOMMENDED READING

Axline, Virginia, *Dibs in Search of Self*, Penguin, 1964.

Beatie, Melody, *Codependant No More*, Harper-Hazelden, 1987.

Bennett, Rita, *Emotionally Free*, Revell, 1982.

Cleese, John and Skynner, Robin, *Families and How to Survive Them*, Methuen, 1983.

Fraiberg, Selma, *The Magic Years*, Charles Scribner & Sons, New York, 1959.

Hurding, Roger, *Roots and Shoots*, Hodder and Stoughton, 1985.

Laing, R.D., *The Divided Self*, Penguin, 1988.

Lake, Frank, *Clinical Theology* (abridged version), Darton, Longman & Todd, 1986.

Lake, Frank, *Tight Corners in Pastoral Counselling*, Darton, Longman & Todd, 1981.

Linn, Dennis and Matthew, *Healing Life's Hurts*, Paulist Press, 1978.

MacNutt, Francis, *Healing*, Hodder and Stoughton, 1989.

MacNutt, Francis, *Praying for Your Unborn Child*, Hodder & Stoughton, 1988.

Martin, Ralph, *Husbands, Wives, Parents, Children*, Servant Books, Michigan, 1978.

Montagu, Ashley, *Touching*, Harper-Row, 1971.

Patterson, Evelyn, *Who Cares?*, Morehouse-Barlow, 1982.

Payne, Leanne, *The Broken Image*, Crossway Books, 1981.

Payne, Leanne, *Crisis in Masculinity*, Kingsway, 1988.

Powell, John, *Will the Real Me Please Stand Up*, Tabor Pub., 1985.

Powell, John, *Fully Human, Fully Alive*, Argus Communications, 1976.

Sandford, John and Paula, *Transformation of the Inner Man*, Bridge Publishing, 1982.

Seamans, David, *Healing for Damaged Emotions*, Victor Books, 1982.

Seamans, David, *Putting Away Childish Things*, Victor Books, 1984.

Scott Peck, M., *The Road Less Travelled*, Simon & Schuster, N.Y., 1978.

Skynner, Robin, *One Flesh, Separate Persons*, Constable, 1976.

Verney, Thomas, *The Secret Life of the Unborn Child*, Delta, 1981.

REFERENCES

Introduction

1. *A Master of the Marionettes* (BBC 1, 18.4.89).
2. J. Bowlby, *The Making and Breaking of Affectional Bonds*, Tavistock Publications, London, 1979, p.20.
3. Henri J.M. Nouwen, *Reaching Out*, Collins, Glasgow, 1975, p. 88.

Chapter 1

1. Ralph Martin, *Husbands, Wives, Parents, Children*, Servant Books, Ann Arbor, Michigan, 1978, p. 117.
2. John Powell, *Will the Real Me Please Stand Up*, Tabor Publishing, Allen, TX. Valencia, CA, 1985, p. 175.
3. Thomas Verney, M.D., *The Secret Life of the Unborn Child*, Delta Publishing, New York, 1981, p. 152.
4. Ashley Montagu, *Touching*, Harper & Row, New York, 1971, p. 98.
5. Thomas Verney, op. cit., p. 164.
6. Madeleine Davis and David Wallbridge, *Boundary and Space*, Penguin, Harmondsworth, 1981, p. 56.
7. J. Bowlby, *The Making and Breaking of Affectional Bonds*, Tavistock Publications, London, 1979, p.48.
8. Charles L. Whitfield, *Healing the Child Within*, Health Communications, Inc., Deerfield Beach, Florida, 1987, p. 71.
9. Ibid., p. 86.
10. Alice Miller, *The Drama of Being a Child*, Virago, London, 1987, p. 62.

11. Robin Skynner, *One Flesh, Separate Persons*, Constable, London, 1976, p. 39.

Chapter 2

1. Robin Skynner, *One Flesh, Separate Persons*, Constable, London, 1976, p. 146.
2. Ibid., p. 108.

Chapter 3

1. Francis and Judith MacNutt, *Praying for the Unborn Child*, Hodder & Stoughton, London, 1988, p. 44.
2. Frank Lake, *Tight Corners in Pastoral Counselling*, Darton, Longman & Todd, London, 1981, p. 15.
3. Ibid., p. x.
4. Thomas Verney, *The Secret Life of the Unborn Child*, p. 77.
5. Ibid., p. 79.
6. Ibid., p. 12.
7. Ibid., p. 95.
8. Francis and Judith MacNutt, op. cit., p. 114.
9. Frank Lake, op. cit., p. 16.

Chapter 4

1. Frank Lake, *Tight Corners in Pastoral Counselling*, pp. 18–19.
2. Francis and Judith MacNutt, *Praying for your Unborn Child*, p. 13.
3. Thomas Verney, *The Secret Life of the Unborn Child*, p. 87.
4. Charles L. Whitfield, *Healing the Child Within*, p. 71.
5. Frank Lake, op. cit., p. 19.
6. Ibid., p. 20.
7. Thomas Verney, op. cit., p. 101.
8. Ibid., p. 102.
9. Ibid., p. 104.
10. Francis and Judith MacNutt, op. cit., p. 102.

Chapter 5

1. Robin Skynner, *Explorations with Families*, Methuen, London, 1987, p. 271.
2. Thomas Verney, *The Secret Life of the Unborn Child*, p. 157.
3. Selma H. Fraiberg, *The Magic Years*, Charles Scribner & Sons, New York, 1959, p. 70.
4. Ashley Montagu, *Touching*, p. 79.
5. Ibid.
6. Morten Kelsey, *The Christian and the Supernatural*, Augsburg, Minneapolis, 1976, p. 33.
7. Robin Skynner, op. cit., p. 271.
8. J. Bowlby, *The Making and Breaking of Affectional Bonds*, p. 114.
9. Robin Skynner, *One Flesh, Separate Persons*, p. 29.
10. Robin Skynner, *Explorations with Families*, p. 130.
11. Michael Jacobs, *Towards the Fullness of Christ*, Darton, Longman & Todd, London, 1988, p. 29.
12. Frank Lake, *Tight Corners in Pastoral Counselling*, p. 102.
13. Frank Lake, *Clinical Theology* (abridged by Martin H. Yeomans), Darton, Longman & Todd, London, 1986, p. 108.
14. Alison Miller, *Daily Telegraph*, 24 Jan. 1989.
15. Erik Erikson, *Childhood and Society*, Paladin Grafton Books, London, 1977, p. 69.
16. John White, *The Masks Of Melancholy*, Inter-Varsity Press, Leicester, 1982, p. 112.

Chapter 6

1. *Concise Oxford Dictionary*.
2. Robin Skynner, *One Flesh, Separate Persons*, p. 30.
3. Ibid., p. 27.
4. Michael Jacobs, *Towards the Fullness of Christ*, Darton, Longman & Todd, London, 1988, p. 123.
5. J. Bowlby, *The Making and Breaking of Affectional Bonds*, p. 132.
6. Robin Skynner, op. cit., p. 30.
7. J. Bowlby, op. cit., p. 108.

8. Madeleine Davis and David Wallbridge, *Boundary and Space*, p. 136.
9. Robin Skynner and John Cleese, *Families and How to Survive Them*, Methuen, London, 1983.
10. Robin Skynner, *Explorations with Families*, p. 273.
11. J. Bowlby, op. cit., p. 10.
12. Ibid.
13. Ibid.
14. Kenneth Rose, *Curzon: A Most Superior Person*, Macmillan, 1985.

Chapter 7

1. Madeleine Davis and David Wallbridge *Boundary and Space*, p. 138.
2. Leanne Payne, *Crisis in Masculinity*, Kingsway Publications, Eastbourne, 1988.
3. Selma H. Fraiberg, *The Magic Years*, p. 204.
4. Robin Skynner, *Explorations with Families*, p. 275.
5. Robin Skynner and John Cleese, *Families and How to Survive Them*, p. 270.
6. Robin Skynner, *One Flesh, Separate Persons*, p. 132.
7. Leanne Payne, *The Broken Image*, Crossway Books, Westchester, Illinois, 1981, p. 43.
8. Leanne Payne, *Crisis in Masculinity*, p. 26.

Chapter 8

1. W. Shakespeare, *As You Like It*, II, vi.
2. Selma Fraiberg, *The Magic Years*, p. 289.
3. Ibid., p. 302.
4. J. Bowlby, *The Making and Breaking of Affectional Bonds*, p. 107.
5. Richard Lovelace, 'To Althea, from Prison'.
6. Selma Fraiberg, op. cit., p. 147.
7. Ibid., p. 275.
8. Ibid., p. 278.

9. Charles L. Whitfield, *Healing the Child Within*, p. 44.
10. J. Bowlby, op. cit., p. 116.

Chapter 9

1. Madeleine Davis and David Wallbridge, *Boundary and Space*, p. 95.
2. James Dobson, *Parenting Isn't for Cowards*, Word (UK) Ltd., Milton Keynes, 1988, p. 143.
3. Ibid.
4. Leanne Payne, *Crisis in Masculinity*, p. 87.
5. Helena Wilkinson, *Puppet on a String*, Hodder & Stoughton, London, 1984, p. 39.
6. Madeleine Davis and David Wallbrige, op. cit., p. 93.
7. Michael Jacobs, *Towards the Fullness of Christ*, Darton, Longman & Todd, London, 1988, p. 108.
8. James Dobson, op. cit., p. 152.
9. Leanne Payne, *The Broken Image*, p. 57.
10. Leanne Payne, *Crisis in Masculinity*, p. 88.
11. James Dobson, op. cit., p. 159.
12. Madeleine Davis and David Wallbridge, op. cit., p. 142.
13. Leanne Payne, *The Broken Image*, p. 58.
14. Floyd McClung, Jr, *The Father Heart of God*, Harvest House, Eugene, Oregon 97402, 1985, p. 34.

Mary Pytches

SET MY PEOPLE FREE

The demand for the Christian ministry of inner healing has
grown rapidly in recent years. The new release of the Holy
Spirit's power in many churches is uncovering buried hurts
and fears, bringing wholeness to lives marred by broken
relationships, wrong values and past pain.

What exactly is this ministry? Who can it help? And how
can it be started? Mary Pytches answers these questions from
personal experience, having undergone the healing of hurts
in her own life, and having spent nine years ministering inner
healing to others at St Andrew's, Chorleywood, where her
husband David is vicar.

Her guidelines are concise, practical and deeply caring, and
will encourage ordinary Christians who want to be healed
and who long to mediate this healing to others.

Mary Pytches

A HEALING FELLOWSHIP

What makes for 'safe' counselling? What boundaries and limits must be built around the counselling relationship? How do you distinguish between demonisation and psychological trauma? Is inner healing biblical?

Drawing on her years of counselling experience at St Andrew's, Chorleywood, Mary Pytches provides practical guidelines for any church or individual wishing to enter into this ministry. The importance of the church community is emphasised whilst she looks in detail at the nature of the relationship between counsellor and counsellee. Mary Pytches describes the need for a 'safe place' to be found in which counselling can occur. St Andrew's is seeking to be a true community where – in today's hurting world – fellowship and healing may be found.

Barry Kissell

ANOTHER WAY

Another Way is a compelling call to rediscover the power of the Cross as the Church continues to experience renewal. With illustrations from St Andrew's, Chorleywood, and from many other churches, Barry Kissell shows how the Cross is the place where fellowship with God is established. He also shows its significance as its power deals with unforgiveness, illness, demonisation and broken fellowship.

Whether it is sharing the faith, discipleship or the healing ministry, 'I have tried to show that in every aspect the Cross offers the disciple of Jesus "another way" ', writes Barry Kissell. This way inevitably involves suffering . . . including that involved in leading a congregation into renewal.

The Rev Barry Kissell travels all over the world with his faith-sharing teams from St Andrew's, Chorleywood in Hertfordshire. He is the author of *Walking on Water*.